George Forrest Browne

Augustine and his Companions

Four Lectures delivered at St. Paul's in January, 1895

George Forrest Browne

Augustine and his Companions
Four Lectures delivered at St. Paul's in January, 1895

ISBN/EAN: 9783337176211

Printed in Europe, USA, Canada, Australia, Japan

Cover: Foto ©ninafisch / pixelio.de

More available books at **www.hansebooks.com**

AUGUSTINE
AND HIS COMPANIONS.

Four Lectures

DELIVERED AT ST. PAUL'S IN JANUARY, 1895,

BY THE

RIGHT REV. G. F. BROWNE, B.D., D.C.L.,
CANON OF ST. PAUL'S; FORMERLY DISNEY PROFESSOR OF ARCHAEOLOGY IN
THE UNIVERSITY OF CAMBRIDGE; BISHOP OF STEPNEY.

PUBLISHED UNDER THE DIRECTION OF THE TRACT COMMITTEE.

LONDON:
SOCIETY FOR PROMOTING CHRISTIAN KNOWLEDGE,
NORTHUMBERLAND AVENUE, W.C.; 43, QUEEN VICTORIA STREET, E.C.
BRIGHTON: 129, NORTH STREET.
NEW YORK: E. & J. B. YOUNG & CO.
1895.

Oxford
HORACE HART, PRINTER TO THE UNIVERSITY

PREFACE.

I SEE that in an interesting review in the Leiden *Theol. Tijdschrift* (Maar., 1895) of my last year's course of lectures at St. Paul's, *The Church in these Islands before the coming of Augustine*, a very friendly Dutch critic thinks that my "Exkurs" on Pelagius and Coelestius "schijnt hier misplaatst." Considering that my one purpose was to speak of the Britons and the Celts, and that one of these was a Briton and the other a Celt, and that both of them play highly important parts in Church History, I cannot quite agree with my critic. I should not have referred to this, however, if it had not provided an opportunity for a more general remark. My wish has been, all through, to put as much material and as many collateral points and illustrations as possible into my lectures. It seems to me important that the early British and English periods should be made to look large and full, and should be linked as completely as may be with the general swing and go of the then world. No doubt the attempt to carry out this purpose gives at times a sense of crowdedness, and at times a sense of delay in coming to the point. These objections I have intentionally disregarded. I need scarcely add that to have allowed them to prevail would have saved me some hours of work and many risks of error.

G. F. STEPNEY.

CONTENTS.

LECTURE I.

Preludes of the English Church. — Modern Roman controversy. — Gregory and the Yorkshire boys. — An earlier suggestion of missionary work in England. — English slaves in Rome. — Patrimony of St. Peter. — Purchase of English boys. — Mission of Augustine. — The missionaries wish to turn back. — Gregory sends them on. — They sail for England. — Richborough. — Their landing-place. — Gregory's object. — King Ethelbert. — Lord Granville's cross. — The Conference. — They enter Canterbury . **7-50**

PAGES

LECTURE II.

Their manner of life. — St. Martin's, Canterbury. — Baptism of Ethelbert. — Miracles. — Consecration of Augustine. — Arles and Vienne. — Foreign consecrations of English bishops and archbishops. — Profession of obedience by English bishops. — State of the see of Rome. — Augustine's questions to Gregory; liturgies, marriage, consecration of bishops, the bishops of Britain. — Success in Kent. — Arrival of more missionaries; books and vestments. — The Charter of the English Church. — Succession of bishops. — Metropolitans and the pallium. — National customs. — Gregory's letter to Ethelbert 51-95

LECTURE III.

A cathedral church built. — First conference with the Britons. — Welsh monasteries and bishoprics. — Second conference; failure. — Bishoprics of London and Rochester. — Endowments. — Death of Augustine. — Dedications of Churches; St. Martin, Christ Church, St. John Baptist, St. Peter and St. Paul (St. Pancras), St. Mary, St. Andrew, St. Paul 96-148

LECTURE IV.

The Canterbury succession. — Laurentius and the Scots. — Mellitus sent by Laurentius to Rome. — Death of Ethelbert. — Paganism of Eadbald and of Sabert's sons. — Flight of Italian bishops to Gaul. — Their return. — Death of Laurentius. — Succession and death of Mellitus. — Succession of Justus. — The pallium again sent. — The conversion of Northumbria. — Consecration of Honorius by Paulinus. — Conversion of the East Angles. — Death of Edwin and flight of Paulinus. — Net result of the Italian Mission. — Act for restraining Appeals to Rome 149-191

Note on Co Consecrators 192, 193
Note on the Pallium 194-201

AUGUSTINE AND HIS COMPANIONS.

LECTURE I.

Preludes of the English Church. — Modern Roman controversy. — Gregory and the Yorkshire boys. — An earlier suggestion of missionary work in England. — English slaves in Rome. — Patrimony of St. Peter. — Purchase of English boys. — Mission of Augustine. — The missionaries wish to turn back. — Gregory sends them on. — They sail for England. — Richborough. — Their landing-place. — Gregory's object. — King Ethelbert. — Lord Granville's cross. — The Conference. — They enter Canterbury.

A YEAR ago, we considered the Church in these islands before the coming of Augustine. We brought the history down to the time when the English people had driven the Britons and their Christianity to the west of the island, had settled themselves down in their new possessions, and had become ripe for the introduction of Christianity. We left our English ancestors just at the point when all that was needed was some one to touch the spring that should launch the Church of England. And we saw that the man was ready, Gregory the Bishop of Rome —Gregory the Great as he is called for reasons far different from this, Gregory the Great as he must have been to us at least, even if the whole Christian world had not so distinguished him.

On that occasion we cleared the ground of much that we must otherwise have considered now. We went at some length into the facts and surmises respecting Bertha, the Christian queen of the pagan king of Kent, and her chaplain-bishop, Luidhard, who kept up Christian worship for her at St. Martin's, Canterbury. We saw that in all probability his ministrations lasted through many years, lasted till near the time at which we have now arrived, when they were ended by his death at Canterbury. And we credited him with being the medium of communication with the Christian priests of the neighbouring parts, no doubt of Gaul[1], to whom, as

---

[1] For some of the reasons for this conclusion, as against the alternative view that the priests or bishops of the Britons are meant, see *The Christian Church in these Islands before the coming of Augustine*, S.P.C.K., 2nd ed., p. 24. It

Gregory tells us in his letters (vi. 58; vi. 59) to the Kings Theoderic and Theodebert, and to Queen Brunichild [1], word had come that the English people earnestly desired to become Christians. The priests, however, or bishops, as some interpret *sacerdotes*, neglected the call, and took no pastoral interest in the wishes of the English.

We have now to deal with Gregory's own personal share in the accomplishment of the work which was thus neglected. We may regard it as a very fortunate thing, that the local neglect had the result of connecting England, in its earliest Christian times, with the great centre of Western civilisation and of Catholic and Apostolic truth. The pleasure of speaking thus of Rome, as it then on the whole was, will be sadly marred when we have to make reference to the Rome of later times, fallen from her high estate of faith and of practice.

And, indeed, I will not refrain from ex-

may be added that in both the letters in which this fact is mentioned Gregory, in the next sentence but one, uses exactly the same phrase, *e vicino*, for the priests with whom the Frankish kings were to provide Augustine. The other matters referred to above are discussed at pp. 9–26 of that little book.

[1] Or Brunehaut.

pressing a feeling which is prominent in my mind when I contemplate the task before me. Years ago it would have been all pleasant, the following step by step the progress of a noble work; noting here and there the weaknesses which were then as now a part of human nature, even in its higher developments; the failures which then sometimes attended, as now they attend sometimes, the best directed exertions; the grave failures attending then as now exertions ill directed. To follow the steps of the pioneers throughout with loving if discriminating sympathy, both for the sake of themselves and for the sake of that which now in the lateness of time we owe to them, that would indeed have been a pleasant task. But a baleful shadow has been cast upon the process by the recrudescence of a controversy forced upon us from without; forced upon us by the modern representatives of the Church to which in Gregory's time we owed our actual beginning, from which in mediaeval times the English Church and England suffered tyranny and extortion that seem to us now equally monstrous and ridiculous. Early Rome was a blessing to England; mediaeval Rome was in part a blessing, in greater part a curse;

modern Rome has in this last year or two become openly a firebrand. We are now in January, 1895. In January, 1825, the preparations were being made which came to a head the next month, when the principal Roman Catholics of England and Ireland made such declarations, and agreed to such oaths, as gained for them a generous recognition and hospitality. That this recognition was fully accorded we may well be thankful; while at the same time we may feel that the aggressive action of individuals, so contrary to the solemn declarations which earned this full recognition, has, in the case of individuals, forfeited such part of it as may be of individual and personal application. But not all the attempts of the aggressive modern Roman, to do all the harm he can to the national Church of England, shall have any effect to modify the frankness of my gratitude to the men who were the spiritual ancestors alike of him and of us.

You are all of you familiar with the story, so often told, so often to be told again, of the first recorded meeting of Gregory with an Englishman. The news spread in Rome one day that some merchants had arrived with many things for sale from distant parts.

The people flocked to the market-place, among them Gregory, not yet Pope. It has been suggested that the place was the Forum of Trajan, a short mile from Gregory's home on the western slope of the Caelian Hill. He saw put up for sale some young men; the tradition at Canterbury said they were three[1]. He was attracted by their appearance; they were fair, handsome, with beautiful hair— "noble heads of hair," the Saxon homily says[2]. He accosted their owners, enquiring whence the youths came. "From the island of Britain," was the reply of the merchants; "that is the type of the people there."—"Are the islanders Christians or Pagans?" was the next question. It was a curiously ignorant question, in face of the assertion of the modern Roman of London that St. Peter founded the Christian Church in these islands, and that the Britons were Roman Catholics. Rome would seem to have kept little count of her flock and their fortunes and misfortunes, their sufferings at the hands of the pagan Saxons. We, however, with history, are fairer to Gregory and to Rome. "They are Pagans," was the answer.—"Alas," sighed Gregory,

[1] Thorn, p. 1757.
[2] Elstob, *Homily on Gregory's birthday*, p. 11.

"shame on us, that such lightsome countenances should be subject to the author of darkness; such graceful forms should be so void of inward grace!"—"How is their nation called?" "They are called Angles." "That is well called; for they have the face of angels[1], and are meet to be fellow-heirs with the angels in heaven."—"How do you call their territory?" "It is called Deira[2]." "That is well called; *de ira*, from the wrath of God, they shall be rescued."—"How is their king called?" "Ælle."—"Alleluia! Their land shall sing the praise of God their maker!"

Gregory went to the Pope, probably Pela-

---

[1] About 950 years after this, another Italian made this same remark about another English face. The coincidence and the contrast are interesting. When Henry VIII was thirty-seven years of age, the year after his application to the Pope for a declaration that his marriage with Catharine of Arragon was invalid, the Venetian ambassador, Falieri, sent a private account of his appearance and character to his employers. It sets before us a man in all ways noble. As for his face, "his face is like an angel's, so fair it is."

[2] This used to be taken as Deora, the deerland. But it is now agreed that the name is formed from the British Deur, or Deivr. The district roughly corresponded with Yorkshire, between the Humber and the Tees. In the time of the Romans a tribe of Parisi occupied this territory.

gius II (578–590) who immediately preceded him, and proposed a missionary expedition to the English, offering to go himself. Whether he had bought the boys we are not told. But he could not be spared from Rome, and nothing came of it then. The story goes that Gregory, either on this occasion or possibly some not inconsiderable time before this, in his desire to convert the English, stole privately out of Rome, and got some little distance away from the city. At midday, he sat down to rest in a field, and a great insect settled on his book, as insects of an unpleasant character have a habit of doing in hot countries when you provide for them a shady place. "Ah!" he said to himself, "*locusta*, a locust; *loco sta*, stay where you are; I must not leave Rome." And he returned.

There are references in one of Gregory's letters to an influence, in the direction of the conversion of the English, from an unexpected quarter. In a letter (viii. 30) to Eulogius the Patriarch of Alexandria, of whom he had evidently the very highest opinion, he says more than once that the prayers of Eulogius had moved him to attempt the conversion of the English. It seems clear that he refers to requests and prayers relating directly to the

English people, not merely urging him to missionary enterprise. I do not know that the cause of this intervention of Eulogius is now traceable. In this same letter, by the way, Gregory entreats Eulogius never again to speak of him as "commanding" him to do anything, or as a "universal pope." That title he will never accept, for that honour would take away the honour of others, there being many ecclesiastics called popes. Eulogius, for instance, he remarks, when he called Gregory "universal pope," practically denied that he himself was that which he declared Gregory wholly to be; the epithet "universal," "universal pope," left no room for any other to be called pope, and that he could never allow. His letters to John (e. g. v. 18), the Patriarch of Constantinople, against the assumption of the title "universal bishop," are more often quoted. The title of universal bishop, he declares, as though he saw, through the centuries, the arrogancy of his own successors, was in itself pestiferous and profane; its assumption indicated the near approach of antichrist.

I have said that the cause of the intervention of Eulogius may not be traceable. But I will venture to make a suggestion.

Anything that may tend to go to the origin of the impulse to which we owe the English Church must have an interest for us.

We learn from a passage in Procopius, quoted by Mr. Freeman in his *Norman Conquest*[1], that in the time of the Emperor Justinian, who reigned from 527 to 565, the king of the Franks sent an embassy to the Emperor at Constantinople. The embassy consisted of some of the Franks near the king's person; and along with them he sent some of the Angles, assuming the air of overlord of their island. Now Eulogius became Patriarch of Alexandria in 579, having for some considerable time previously been the head of the monastery of the Deipara at Antioch. He was no doubt often in Constantinople in the time of Justinian; indeed, as he became Patriarch eleven years before Gregory became Pope of Rome, and Gregory was born about 540, Eulogius may well have been in Constantinople at the time of the Fifth General Council, in 553. Thus it is very possible that Eulogius saw and conversed with the Angles who went on the Frankish embassy, and talked about them to Gregory, when he made his acquaintance

[1] i. 30.

some years later at Constantinople, either before or soon after 579. Gregory himself was in residence at Constantinople, as representative of the Pope, within twelve or thirteen years of Justinian's death. Eulogius, as we know from Gregory's letters, was deeply interested in missions to the heathen. Thus many reasons combine to suggest that here we have the real first impulse towards the creation of the English Church. If that be so, then not the British Church only, but the English Church too, owes itself to the East, looks to the foundation-land of Christianity. And if we put the Frankish embassy late in the reign of Justinian—early it could not well be—it may be that just when young Ethelbert came to the throne, and tried his wings against Wessex, and sent to the nearest Frankish king for a wife, just at that very time the Providence of God was laying in Constantinople the train which in process of time sent Augustine to the king of Kent.

The Saxon homily on Gregory's birthday tells us that the merchants who had the boys for sale were themselves English. The idea of English men taking English boys to Rome to be sold as slaves is at first sight startling.

The demand for slaves had at one time in the history of Rome been so abundantly met, and more than met, by the scores of thousands of captives taken in war, that a slave cost almost nothing, at least in the camp. But for long before the time of which we are speaking the Roman arms had been less prosperous, and slaves taken by Roman armies had ceased to meet the demand. Property of this character was in great request, and a large number of people were concerned in feeding the Roman market by supplies from various parts of the world. In some nations it was the practice to sell off the superfluous children as slaves; this is recorded, for instance, of the non-Greek inhabitants of Phrygia, the Galatian traders being particularly busy in this traffic. But we need not credit our early forefathers with making merchandise of well-grown sons like these, for whom they had plenty of use in their new home, in the country of their conquest. We can explain the fact in a less unnatural manner.

The Ælle of whom Gregory was told was a well-known person in our early history. He was a man as great in carving out a powerful kingdom in the north, as Ethelbert of Kent was in consolidating his dominion in the south; and in the course of time the son of the one married the daughter of the other. It is a singular good fortune that the very first name of an Englishman to fall on the ears of Gregory should be that of a man so intimately connected with the first founders of the two metropolitan sees, Canterbury and York. We have no reason to suppose that Gregory ever followed up in after times his early enquiries about the district from which the slaves came and their king. He died twenty years before Ethelbert's daughter married Ælle's son Edwin, and carried Christianity to the home of these Yorkshire boys.

According to the Anglo-Saxon genealogies —and we make a great mistake when we reject such records—Ælle was ninth in descent from Wægdæg, son of Woden; Ethelbert of Kent was eighth from Vecta, a brother of Wægdæg; and Æthelric of Bernicia was ninth from Bældæg, yet another brother. Ethelbert was the fifth king of Kent; Æthelric's father Ida was the first king of Bernicia; and Ælle had come latest of all, and conquered the Britons of the parts we call Lancashire and Yorkshire, and made himself a king, king of the British Deur; in Latin Deira. These three sets of ninth cousins, finding themselves, after all these generations, fellow-kings in an island which their common ancestor probably never knew, became closely connected by the marriages of Ælle's children; his son Edwin marrying Ethelbert's daughter and his daughter Acca marrying Æthelric's son. We shall see further on that this latter marriage did not bring peace but war. I only mention it here because to this war we probably owe the presence of the Yorkshire boys in Rome.

The interview of the slave-merchants with Gregory probably took place after 585, for it was only then that he returned from his residence of some years in Constantinople, where he had filled the important office of representative of the Bishop of Rome. In 588, Æthelric of Bernicia—that is, the territory between the Forth and the Tees—invaded Deira; Ælle died at an advanced age; and his son Edwin, the young brother of Æthelric's daughter-in-law, was carried off to a place of safety, escaping westwards, where we shall find him later on. It was presumably in this war that the Deiran youths were taken prisoners, and the merchants had not heard that Ælle was dead. Ælle, however, is said by others to have lived to 593.

We must now come to the actual mission

of Augustine, when Gregory had been Bishop of Rome some five years.

The Bishops of Rome held property in various countries, acquired from time to time, out of the revenues of which the poor were maintained[1]. This kind of property was called by the general name of "the patrimony of St. Peter." Gregory paid special attention to it, and gave minute directions for its more profitable management. The estates lay in Etruria, Campania, Corsica, Sicily, Dalmatia, and Africa. A portion of the patrimony was in the neighbourhood of Marseilles, and Gregory had at first left it to the management of the Frankish governor (*Praefectus Galliarum*) of the province of Arles. We have a letter of his, dated 593, acknowledging the receipt of 400 Gallic shillings (*solidi*), and announcing a present in recognition of the governor's care—a cross studded with relics of St. Peter's chains, and set in a portion of the gridiron of St. Lawrence.

Two years after this, if 595 be the right date, Gregory sent Candidus[2], one of his own

---

[1] Kellett, *Gregory the Great, and his relations with Gaul*, Cambridge University Press, 1889, p. 32.

[2] Candidus came back to Rome and was Abbat of St. Andrew's; Greg. *Ep.* viii. 11.

trained priests, to take charge of the patrimony at Marseilles[1]. He bids Candidus spend the receipts, so far as they were paid in Gallic shillings, which, it seems, were worth little in Rome, on either of two objects, clothes for the poor, and English boys of seventeen or eighteen years of age, who might be trained in monasteries to the service of God[2]. And as all who could be found there—apparently the boys were to be bought in England itself—were pagans, a priest was to travel with them, to baptize any who might seem to be dying. The arrangement gives a painfully vivid idea of the trade in human flesh.

It is usually said that Gregory had intended to make of these boys native missionaries for England; and not finding the plan answer, made a more definite attempt upon the work on which he had set his heart. But in fact there was not time for the plan either to succeed or to fail. In that same year, 595,

---

[1] Haddan and Stubbs, iii. 6, and notes in Migne, p. 799.
[2] This rather supports the suggestion on p. 14, that Gregory may have bought the Yorkshire boys whom he saw in Rome, and trained them as Christians. But in that case they soon died; otherwise they would certainly have been sent with Augustine, and interpreters would have been unnecessary.

he matured and set in operation a fresh plan, no less than the mission from Rome of a considerable party of men of position, for the conversion of the English. They were to act under the leadership of Augustine, the prior of the monastery of St. Andrew's in Rome, which Gregory had himself founded on his own property on the Caelian Hill, and had himself ruled as abbat. Of this spot, so vitally interesting to Englishmen from its close connection with Gregory and Augustine, I shall say something in my next lecture, when we come to consider the dedications of churches in England by Augustine and his immediate companions.

In the year 595, just 1300 years ago, but probably rather late in the autumn, there was a lull in the hostility of the Lombards, who could have barred the journey by land, and the missionary party set out from Rome for England. When they had accomplished but a small part of the journey, so Bede describes it, they became afraid. In all probability they had got further than Bede's phrase would suggest, had crossed the Alps, and reached Aix in Provence, or Lérins the famous island off the south coast of Gaul. The state of Gaul was in itself enough to frighten them.

Accustomed, as we are, to think of France as one, we cannot without serious difficulty realise what Gaul then was, with its divisions and their internecine strife. Five centuries after this, it was still so far from being one, that Anselm, on his way from England to Rome, treated as a hero in one province, had to travel incognito in another. That, however, was due to the divisions of Christendom. It is a homily on the ineffable unity which men are told they find and always found in submitting themselves to Rome. There were two violently opposing centres of this perfect unity, sole centres, the one with his fighting followers entrenched in the Lateran fortress, the other in garrison in the Castle of St. Angelo. In the parts of France where Urban was Pope, there Anselm was a hero, and went proudly; where Clement was Pope, there he hid his face and got quietly out of a very real danger. In Augustine's time the dangers of the way through Gaul were caused by the violence of opposing princes, or rather, a still worse thing in those times when it happened, the violence of the women who guided the princes. The very names of Frédégonde, who reigned by murder in the western half of Gaul, and of Brunehaut, whose grandsons, still minors, were supposed to rule respectively in Burgundy, the southern half of eastern France, and Austrasia, the northern half, were enough to frighten ordinary people; and those years, 595 and 596, were fateful years with those murderous Merovingian matrons. And, further, Augustine and his companions had now come near enough to learn a little more about the manners and customs of the handsome fair-haired race, whose boys had been found so picturesque in swarthy Rome. "Manners makyth man." They were barbarous, ferocious, obstinate unbelievers. Better go back home than go to them. That was the direction in which the mind of one and another of the mission band was turning. When they came to discuss the matter openly, it was found to be the common opinion among them that it was safer to go back. That is the word by which Bede expresses it, *tutius*, more safe. How many a noble work would never have been done, how many a triumph for Christ would never have been accomplished, if this unmissionary word had been found in the missionary's dictionary.

No sooner said than done. Augustine was sent back at once to Rome, to beg of Gregory, with humble supplication, that they should not be held bound to proceed on an expedition so dangerous, so laborious, so uncertain. That was the order of the epithets.

Gregory sent Augustine back to them with a written answer. It is preserved to us by Bede, who got copies of the letters on the English mission, written from and to Rome, from our London Archpresbyter Nothelm, who went to Rome for the purpose. The letter ran thus—"It were better not to enter upon good deeds, than to turn back from them. Carry out, with the utmost zeal, the good work which by the Lord's help you have begun. The labour, the abuse, of which you tell me, disregard. Great labours for God receive a greater and eternal weight of glory. To complete this work will be to the everlasting profit of your souls."

And then there came a passage in the letter which shews the skill of a practical man. Nothing has been said by Bede which gives any hint that Augustine had been a dissentient, when the opinion of the body of monks was taken. But Gregory sends him back to the work as though there was no doubt about his zeal and determination. "When Augustine, your provost, returns to you, whom I have now made your abbat, obey him humbly in all things."

So Augustine joined his companions again. He brought with him other letters from Gregory, to be delivered to important people at various stages of the journey; so selected, apparently, as to cover either of two possible routes, the one going as far east as Metz, the other keeping to the west of this, by Châlons and Soissons. So far as the map is concerned, it was possible to avoid Neustria, the western division, and the more dangerous, and yet embark at one of the three ports in the near neighbourhood of Boulogne. But the ordinary routes passed through portions of Frédégonde's territory, and one of Gregory's letters of introduction was addressed to the Bishop of Tours, almost the centre of Neustria. Gregory's letters to some of the secular potentates have brought upon him the reproach of writing in highly complimentary terms to people whose lives he must have abhorred. The letters of Popes to evil sovereigns are not particularly pleasant reading. If it is true that people have to eat a peck of dirt before they die, they need not eat so much in one letter.

Bede, in the opening sentences of his Ecclesiastical History of the English race, where he describes the size and situation of the island of Britain, formerly called Albion as he tells us, remarks that the city called the Port of Rutubis is that which first opens to travellers crossing the sea from Belgic Gaul; and he gives its distance from Boulogne as fifty miles, in his opinion, though others called it fifty-five. This seems to shew that he regarded Boulogne as the natural point of departure for Augustine. Quentavic, the modern Étaples, some miles south of Boulogne, was also used in those days, for instance, by Theodore, as also was the Portus Itius, to the east of Cape Gris Nez.

Leaving Gaul by one of these ports, Augustine and his companions reached this island by the port of Rutubis. This is the modern Richborough; one of the many hints that the broad *u* was by no means universal among the Romans, and that in some cases at least they pronounced *tu* as some English people pronounce it in the word *future*. Rutubis, or Ritupis, as Antonine spells it, may have been pronounced Richŭbis. We find a similar hint in a beautiful inscription now in the Wasserkirche at Zürich, set up in the Roman times by a freedman of Augustus and his wife to their much-loved son, a little boy of one year five months and five days old. It is said to be the only monument known with the Roman form of the name Zürich. The Roman form is Turicum [1].

There are not anywhere in Britain more magnificent remains of the Roman rule than the mighty walls of Richborough. Built in courses of six feet from one horizontal row of tiles to another, they are twelve feet thick, and in parts still from thirty to forty feet high. The north wall is 560 feet long. They form three sides of a rectangle, enclosing a space of seven acres. The water front is sufficiently defended by the cliff, as it seems; but experts feel no doubt that a wall ran

[1] This inscription is in more than one way both interesting and remarkable. I give it as throwing a pleasant light upon the affectionateness of domestic life among some at least of the Romans, in the second century after Christ.

HIC SITVS EST L. AEL. VRBICVS QVI VIXIT AN. VNO M. V D. V VNIO AVG. LIB. P. P. STA. TVRICEN. XL G. ET AELIA SECVND P DVLCISSIMO F.

"Here is laid Laelius Aelius Urbicus, who lived one year five months five days. Unio, freedman of Augustus, Provost of the Turican Station for collecting the Gaulish entrance toll of two-and-a-half per cent. on goods, and Aelia Secundina, parents, to their much loved son."

It will be noticed that the freedman's son took his name from his mother's family.

along the edge of the cliff, and has disappeared under the encroachments of the water. The water, however, has retired for centuries.

Within this enclosure there is in the ground a rectangular platform of flint and boulder masonry, 144 feet long and 104 feet broad—the diameter of this dome of St. Paul's is only about 110 feet. This enormous mass of masonry, 5 feet thick, supports a great cruciform superstructure, solid, also 5 feet thick, the cross being 87 feet long and 46 feet along the arms. What was the purpose of this unique structure is a problem yet to be solved. On account of the connection of these noble walls with the first step in the actual commencement of the English Church, the whole site has been purchased and put into the hands of perpetual trustees, at the instance of the Archbishop of Canterbury. There is, outside the walls, a great elliptical amphitheatre, 200 feet long and 166 feet broad, commanding a great view of the approaches by sea and land.

The fortress gave its name to the whole of the harbour, which extended—to use modern names—from Sandwich to Ramsgate, and is now mainly represented, so far as the sea is concerned, by Pegwell Bay. In Augustine's time this great opening in the land passed right through to the north coast of Kent, and was in fact an arm of the sea, which cut off the land to the east from the mainland, and thus formed the Isle of Thanet, now the north-eastern part of the mainland of Kent. The sea has since those times retired, but the ground which represents the old bed of the water is for the most part only six or seven feet above the level of the sea, and nowhere, I think, more than ten feet. The river Stour, flowing quietly down from Canterbury, entered the then expanse of water at a place still called Stourmouth, about midway between its northern and southern extremities. Part of its water thus passed southwards, and was called the Wantsumu, and part passed northwards and was called the Glenlade. Wantsumu was also used as the name of the whole expanse of water. Bede so uses it. At the northern junction with the open sea stood another mighty fortress of the Romans, Regulbium, Reculver. This does not loom so large to the eye now as Richborough does, but on the southern and eastern sides the walls are still twelve feet high, and as massive as those of Richborough. The northern wall, and half the area which the walls enclosed, have been gradually washed away by the undermining action of the sea, and modern skill has only barely succeeded in saving the two picturesque towers of the ancient church. The destruction of the nave and chancel of this church, with their striking Roman architecture, the only remaining example of the division between nave and chancel by an arcade of Roman columns[1], was one of the barbarisms of last century. We have still *in situ* the bases of like columns at the ruins of St. Pancras, in Canterbury, a church which dates before Augustine's time, as we shall see later. Within the enclosure, which, including the thickness of the walls, exceeded eight acres, the ground is up to and above the level of the top of the wall. It is ordinarily said that the ground has risen, from the accumulation of sixteen centuries of débris. But at Richborough there is nothing of the kind. I should venture to suggest, from a close examination of the whole position, that it was originally a very clearly-defined natural mound, which the Romans

---

[1] There is a very striking Roman arcade across the church at Brixworth, near Northampton. Two of the Reculver columns are set up in a garden in the Cathedral precincts at Canterbury.

cut square and protected with walls, built against the vertical sides. Was ever channel guarded by two such magnificent fortresses as these?[1] Ships that would avoid them, on the way to the Thames, must pass round the North Foreland, the promontory of Cantion, Promontorium Acantium.

The name of Northmouth still remains near Reculver, but the waters of the Stour no longer pass out that way. They wander to the south-east, winding with many convolutions through the low-lying ground, and escape into Pegwell Bay. Some idea of the extent of their windings may be gathered from the following fact. At one point of the causeway between Ramsgate in the Isle of Thanet and Sandwich on the mainland—if Sandwich can be so described—there is only just room for the road, between the Stour on one side, running from the marshes to Sandwich, and the Stour on the other side, running from Sandwich to the sea. The loop which the river makes in its course from one side of the road to the other is six miles in

---

[1] The Roman works which still remain in Kent, at Richborough, Reculver, Dover, and Lymne, were in themselves sufficient to make the Romans feel at home there. They did not reach the South Saxons, so they may not have seen the Roman work of Pevensey.

length. It passes on its way under the inland cliff of Richborough and the Bloody Point, where the Danes were met by the men of Sandwich and Stonar 150 years after the period on which our thoughts are bent.

In Bede's time the water between the Isle of Thanet and the mainland was three furlongs across, and was passable—no doubt he means fordable at low water—at two points only. Of these, the present St. Nicholas at Wade, ad Vadum, was beyond doubt one. As to the other, we have a curious piece of evidence. There is a map of the Isle of Thanet in the Manuscript History of St. Augustine's, Canterbury, now in the safe possession of Trinity Hall, Cambridge, written about 1414, and assigned to Thomas of Elmham, a monk of St. Augustine's. The purpose of the map was to shew the course taken by a tame stag from Westgate on the north coast of Thanet to its home on the south of the island, under the following circumstances. King Egbert of Kent, great-grandson of Ethelbert who is to play a large part in our story, had allowed his minister Thunor to murder[1] the real heirs to the throne, Eg-

[1] At Eastry, three and a half miles from Richborough, on the Roman road to Dover.

bert's own cousins, in 664. In expiation, he promised their sister Dompneva[1], the foundress of the monastery which has given its name to Minster in the Isle of Thanet, as much of the island as her tame hind marked out at one run. The map of 1414, which shews the course of the hind, was of course copied from a much earlier map; indeed, the course is so erratic, and its importance as the boundary of a great estate was so real, that we may fairly take the map as a record of great antiquity. At any rate, when it was originally drawn, Thanet was in the fullest sense an island, and the roads running westwards struck the shore at two points only, no doubt the two places referred to by Bede. One is at Sarre, where the roads through Minster and Monkton and the road through St. Nicholas converge. The other is nearly due south from Minster, which was then very near the shore; the railway line from Minster to Sandwich passes over the place. At the former of the two points the map shews a ferry-boat with people in it, and a man with a red cross wading to the island, making for St. Nicholas at Wade. On

[1] She was mother of St. Mildred and daughter of Ermenred, King Eadbald's son.

one or other of these two roads Augustine and his companions certainly walked, when their journey to the capital began. All the probabilities point to the Minster road as that by which they proceeded to leave the island.

Such was the nature of the Rutupian Port, at which Augustine and his companions, about forty in all, arrived safely, some time between the summer of 596 and the early spring of 597. At what point of the long range of low land they disembarked, we do not know.

The prevailing belief of modern times is that the band of missionaries landed at the head of Pegwell Bay, near to Ebbs Fleet, the traditional place of landing of the first of the Jutes, Hengist and Horsa. If any prefer to believe that in the first instance they disembarked on the mainland, at Richborough or at Stonar, there can, I think, be no doubt that they settled themselves on the island, and there awaited the news of the king's will in regard to them. Bede says quite decidedly that they landed on the island, and he received his information about the disciples of Gregory from Abbat Albinus of Canterbury, who sent to him, by the hands or by the mouth of Nothelm the Archpresbyter of London, all that he could learn on the subject from writings or from the traditions of his ancestors. It is, however, the fact that the cliffs and beaches and ports were on the mainland, and there is, so far as I know, no trace of a port on the island side. Probably a quiet bay, with nothing more dangerous than mud and sand, where a ship could run gently ashore at high tide and be left by the receding water, was at least as attractive to the visitors, of whose timidity we have had such evidence, as the bustle of a frequented port. And there is on this supposition a coincidence which we should not like to lose, between the landing-places of the first pagan invaders of the Christian British Cantion and the first Christian invaders of the pagan English Kent.

Another question—With what commission did Augustine come? Did he come in the interests of Rome, to enlarge the area of the claims of the Papacy? Did he come to demand allegiance, homage, to St. Peter, to an infallibly-inspired successor of St. Peter, to the Vicar of Christ on earth, to whom all appeals must come, from whose unerring decision no appeal lay on earth or in heaven? From first to last, in all Gregory's letters, no word of the kind. And yet Augustine was that manner of man that needs a thing to be put very straight to him if he is to take it in. His business was to create an English Church, not to build up an outwork of Rome.

The king of Kent, in whose territory the Italian visitors now found themselves, was Ethelbert, the great-great-grandson of Hengist. As we saw last year, he had married a Christian wife, Bertha, daughter of a former king of the Frankish district, of which Paris was then the capital; Brunehaut and Frédégonde were her uncles' widows. In early youth he had ventured to face the forces of the West Saxons in the battle of Wimbledon, and had been driven back into his own narrow territory. The thirty years that had intervened had seen the further growth of the power of Wessex, and finally its complete collapse. In place of Wessex, Kent had become the dominant power in the south of England. At the same time the Angles in the north had been greatly increasing their power, and they and the men of Kent were the two prominent peoples in the English land. Convert Kent, and convert Northumbria, and England was practically won to Christ. Roughly speaking, Ethelbert, though king of Kent only, was recognised as overlord in the Anglian and Saxon kingdoms of the South Saxons, East Saxons, East Angles, and Mercians. In the case of the East Saxons, who had then quite recently taken London from the British, he had a yet more direct influence, their king Sabert being his sister's son. The East Saxon kingdom, in which we Londoners are concerned, comprised Essex, Middlesex, and Herts.

By Gregory's instructions, Augustine had brought with him to England priests of the Frankish race. They were his interpreters. By their help the Italians were to get at the minds of the English, and by God's goodness help on their will to become Christians. That is Gregory's statement of his purpose [1].

Augustine sent some of his company—no doubt these Frankish priests—to Ethelbert's capital city, the British Dur-wern, Dorovernium, the English Cantwara-byrig, with a message to the king. They had come from Rome, the message ran; and I take it we are listening to the substance of words carefully

---

[1] *Ep.* vi. 58. Queen Bertha's residence in Canterbury would in itself account for the selection of Franks as interpreters to the English king. But there is, as we have seen, evidence of a larger connection than that between the English and the Franks; see p. 16, and p. 9.

considered in Rome by Gregory and Augustine. They had come from Rome. They had brought good tidings, tidings the best and the highest. He who would take to himself, and make his own, the promise of this their message, would have, without any doubt, eternal joys in the heavens, and a kingdom everlasting with God the living and the true.

The king gave attentive audience to the messengers. He bade them tell those who had sent them to remain in the island where they were until he should determine what to do in their case. Meanwhile, their wants should be attended to.

After some days the king came to the island. He seated himself in the open air, and bade Augustine and his companions come to confer with him there. If their purpose was to employ any maleficent art to get the better of him, their purpose would not prevail under the clear sky. That was his view. A conference under a roof might be a different matter.

Where was the conference held, this turning-point in the history of the world, for it was no less than that? One tradition says, at Richborough. If that is so, Bede's expression, Ethelbert "came to the island," must mean came to the shore on the mainland, facing the island—a strained interpretation. It would be better to suppose that Bede's information represented another tradition, which placed the interview on the island itself. The late Earl Granville, who took a great interest in the whole of this district, as Warden of the Cinque Ports, erected a remarkable monument on the site of a great oak tree, which was cut down fifty years before his time. It is half a mile north of Ebbs Fleet, and is close to Cottington Farm, or, as it was called in earlier times, Cotmanfeld, supposed to mean the Field of the Man of God, in reference to Augustine. "Augustine's well" is in a neighbouring field, a pure spring which is said never to fail, rising up in a natural well some four feet deep. The great oak was by tradition the tree under which Ethelbert received Augustine; but in the ancient map of which mention has been made, there is a tree marked in the centre of the island, with two large crosses near it, and it may well have been that the interview took place in this more central place, near the Beacon. It has been objected that these places, whether as landing-places or as places of conference, were under water then. That is true of one of the claimants, the Boarded Groin, which carries confession on its sandy face; but it is not true of the others. The actual spot called Ebbs Fleet, on the right-hand side of the road as you drive from the Halfway House to the Cottington Lane, is only fourteen feet above the sea, that is, only eight feet above the level which represents the bottom of the water in Bede's time. But the ground rises rapidly to Ebbs Fleet Farm, where there must always have been a clearly-defined promontory. The ground rises also, gradually but decidedly, from Pegwell Bay to Cottington Farm, round the back of which the fifty-foot contour line runs.

The monument erected by Lord Granville is a noble cross, with a circular head. It is a conspicuous object from the road between Ramsgate and Sandwich, standing out to the north-west about three and a half miles from the former place. A very interesting and valuable book, recently published, on St. Martin's Church at Canterbury, describes it as an Iona cross, but that would indeed have been an envenomed sarcasm. Lord Granville might as well have represented Augustine with the Celtic tonsure. The great cross at Iona is not of a graceful form, and it differs in two important respects from Lord Granville's cross. The Iona cross has a circular head, but with stiff arms projecting beyond the circle; Lord Granville's has a pure circular outline, a beautiful feature. The Iona cross, like many of the crosses in Ireland, has a very stiff shaft; Lord Granville's shaft has a very graceful entasis. It is in fact a very skilful reproduction of the great crosses at Sandbach in Cheshire—two of the most remarkable monuments of the early times of the English Church. The shaft of the larger of the Sandbach crosses is 16 feet in height, and the circular head, a part of which is still left, was about 4 feet more. With the large base on which the two crosses stand, the top of the higher of the two would be 26 feet from the ground. The shaft of Lord Granville's cross is $11\frac{1}{2}$ feet, and the whole height, including a large base, is $18\frac{1}{2}$ feet. A large number of subjects, very carefully chosen, are represented on the four faces of the shaft and on the head of the cross, and the base bears an inscription written by Dean Liddell, once Lord Granville's tutor. The inscription speaks of the marvellous celerity with which the Christian faith spread through the whole of England, thus striking a note which is not quite in harmony with the lessons I propose to draw from the facts [1].

[1] An excellent account of Earl Granville's Cross, with illustrations of all its faces and a complete description of the subjects, was published at the time by Miss Lucy H. Freeman, then Scholar of Newnham College. Miss Freeman very kindly sent me a copy after a lecture which I gave in Cambridge upon the Sandbach Crosses. The pamphlet can be obtained (price 6*d*.) from the booksellers in Ramsgate; it may properly be described as authorised by the late Earl Granville himself. The inscription is as follows:—

"Augustinus | ad Rutupina littora in insula Thaneti, | post tot terrae marisque labores, | tandem advectus, | hoc in loco cum Ethelberto rege congressus, | primam apud nostrates concionem habuit | et fidem christianam, | quae per totam Angliam mira celeritate diffusa est, | feliciter inauguravit, | A.D. DXCVI. | Quarum Rerum | ut apud Anglos servetur memoria, | hoc monumentum ponendum curavit | G. G. L. G. Comes Granville, Portuum Custos, | A.D. MDCCCLXXXIV."

The following is the authorised translation. Miss Freeman informs us that much consideration was given to the question of the point of disembarcation before Rutupina littora was represented in English by Ebbs Fleet.

"Augustine, at length brought to Ebbs Fleet in the Isle of Thanet, after so many labours on land and at sea, at a conference with King Ethelbert on this spot, delivered his first discourse to our people, and auspiciously founded the Christian faith, which was diffused with wonderful rapidity throughout the whole of England. A.D. 596. In order that the memory of these events may be preserved among the English people, Granville George Leveson-Gower, Earl Granville, Lord Warden of the Cinque Ports, has caused this monument to be erected. A.D. 1884."

The king and Augustine alike can scarce have failed to note, though with very different feelings, the mighty tokens of the earlier work of Rome. Two miles and a half away, towards the noonday sun, stood boldly up the grim walls of Richborough. Clear against the horizon, seven miles to the west, Regulbium shewed itself in its strength. The king's precautionary arrangement for holding the conference in the open air, and not under a roof, gave to the Italian missionaries the opportunity of increasing the solemn effect of their approach. Of that opportunity they availed themselves. Gregory's minute care for the study of church music, and the arrangement of services and ceremonies, told at the very first step in the great work. They came to the king in procession, bearing as their banner a silver cross. The kings of the English knew what it was to have a standard carried before a king. Edwin, who married this man's daughter, even in time of peace always had his banner carried before him, if only for a walk in the streets[1]. Here was the King of Heaven, going forth to peaceful war, and His banner was the cross of Christ; Christ, of whose form they carried with them

[1] Bede ii. 16. The English called it Tuuf.

a representation, painted on a panel, in the grave and dignified manner which marks the saintly delineations of that great century of Christian art. They came on, singing solemn litanies, supplicating the Lord for their own eternal salvation, and the eternal salvation of those for whom, to whom, they had come. Then first the English ear heard the strange rise and fall of the Gregorian Chant, a chant much more severe then than as we know it now, and yet itself a lightening of the still severer Ambrosian strain.

At length the procession reaches the presence. It parts asunder, to the right and the left; and there stands before the king—Augustine: stands tall and gaunt, towering above his companions on this side and on that. In one long look, we may be sure, the eyes of Augustine and of Ethelbert meet; and then Ethelbert, with courteous dignity, bids his visitors be seated. Augustine begins his address; a Frank interprets. When Augustine speaks, with Italian force and fervour, the king, who knows no word of what he says, concentrates his attention upon the personality of the man, the man who in giving his message is so clearly giving his very self;—the personality of the man, that strikes home to the king, as straight as though he knew each word that was said. And then the king turns to the Frankish priest, to learn from him what it is that this striking stranger has poured forth with such depth of conviction. At last the message is told out. The tradition of the English was that it was a very simple message[1]. Just this in substance: "The tenderhearted Healer redeemed by His own death the sinful dwellers on this earth, and opened a way by which they might fare into the kingdom of heaven."

Then the king made answer. Bede, who tells us nothing of what Augustine said, with a true instinct tells us what Ethelbert said. "Fair, indeed, are the words, the promises, you bring to us. But they are new, and not certain. I cannot desert that which for so long a time I, in common with all the English race, have held, to give assent to this new belief. But you have come to me, foreigners, from far. You have come desiring to make known to me also that which, as I seem to myself to have clearly seen, you do verily believe to be true and supremely good. Therefore, I will you not harm. Nay, I receive you, in kindly hospitality. Your needs shall

[1] Haddan and Stubbs, iii. 11.

be my care. And if you find that you can win over to your belief any of my people, I interpose no bar."

Ethelbert immediately carried out his promise of hospitality. He assigned to them a residence in his capital city, the burgh of the Kentish men. We may imagine with what high hope, joyful in so large and early a measure of success, they crossed the water to the mainland and set foot within their ancestral walls, the walls of Richborough, that spoke to them of the Roman occupation. They skirted the walls of the amphitheatre, and paced along the great road that ran and still runs through Ash and Wingham to Canterbury. The last time that Romans had marched with measured tread along that road was 190 years before. They were soldiers, and they marched the reverse way. They were leaving the British land to its fate at the hands of the marauding pagan. The Britons had now disappeared, and the pagan was supreme. The pirates had settled down, and their captains had become kings. The Roman arms had returned, to conquer them to Christ. That was the spirit in which they trode the way that their ancestors had made, with its Roman directness. They came in sight of Canterbury itself, looking down upon it from the hill above St. Martin's. And then began their solemn litany. If Bede's phrase is to be taken strictly, and he is so careful in his statements here that we may fairly suppose that it is, the temporary dwelling-place assigned to them, soon after changed by the king for one more suited to their station, was in the city itself. If that was so, they walked in procession down the hill, singing their litany; turning their eyes to the right-hand side of the road as they passed St. Martin's, taking comfort from the thought that there at least the Christian rites were accustomed to be performed; and almost immediately, but a hundred yards or two lower down, looking askance at the great barrow which still stands by the road side, and the adjoining temple where Ethelbert offered to the gods before his idol. And so at last they came to the city gate and entered in, taking seisin of the English land in the name of Him who is Lord of all. And this was the manner of their going, from the time when they set eyes on the city from St. Martin's hill. We seem to see them bringing out their banners, and forming into line; we seem to hear some one among them, Honorius the future archbishop, or James the perpetual deacon, humming the first note. They bore, as their wont was, the Holy Cross, and the Figure of the great King, our Lord Jesus Christ; and they sang with careful inflections—so well trained were they that they sang as one man, modulated with consonant voice—this litany, which divides itself so clearly into deprecation, confession, thanksgiving: " We humbly pray Thee, O Lord, in all Thy mercy, let Thy wrath and Thine anger be taken away from this city and from Thy holy house, for we have sinned. Alleluia."

LECTURE II.

Their manner of life. — St. Martin's, Canterbury. — Baptism of Ethelbert. — Miracles. — Consecration of Augustine. — Arles and Vienne. — Foreign consecrations of English bishops and archbishops. — Profession of obedience by English bishops. — State of the see of Rome. — Augustine's questions to Gregory; liturgies, marriage, consecration of bishops, the bishops of Britain. — Success in Kent. — Arrival of more missionaries; books and vestments. — The Charter of the English Church. — Succession of bishops. — Metropolitans and the pallium. — National customs. — Gregory's letter to Ethelbert.

LAST week we brought Augustine and his companions to Canterbury, in the year 597, and settled them for a time in the temporary residence provided for them by the king.

They at once began—we cannot do better than follow as closely as may be the actual expressions of Bede—to imitate the apostolical life of the primitive Church. In prayers frequent, in watchings and fastings; preaching the word of life to those whom they could reach; looking upon the things of this world as alien from them; accepting from those whom they taught only the necessaries of life; living completely in accordance with their teaching; being always prepared in mind to suffer any hardships and opposition, even to die, for that truth which they taught. That was Bede's idea of the apostolical life of the primitive Church, 650 years after the Apostles left the earth. It might with advantage be endorsed upon every commission issued for missionary work in our own day.

The ministry of thus teaching by thus living very soon told. Some of the people of the city were attracted by the simplicity of the innocent life of the missionaries, and the sweetness of their heavenly doctrine. They believed, and were baptized. The meeting-place was the old church of St. Martin, outside the walls, on the Richborough road. Here Queen Bertha had been accustomed to attend the ministrations of her chaplain—Bishop Luidhard; and here Augustine, too, and his companions, first met for like purposes; here they sang, prayed, celebrated the mass, preached, and baptized. Bede's phrase is clear—in this church they baptized at first. It was only after the conversion of the king that they received wider permission, to preach where they would, and to build other churches or restore such as still remained from former Christian times.

To this day St. Martin's Church stands. The most complete and careful examination, spread over many years, conducted by the hand and eye of Canon Routledge, and at no inconsiderable cost to him, has revealed facts of the highest interest, both here and at St. Pancras a little further down the hill. There is left, I think, no doubt that the nave of St. Martin's is exactly the original nave, so far as the foundations of the walls are concerned; and that up to a considerable height the walls are themselves the old walls, with Roman plaster still firm and sound on the inside. The chancel has quite recently been discovered to be twice the original length. The walls of the western half of the chancel are the original walls, for some height up, and the square returns of the old east wall have now been found, shewing, so far as they have been followed, no suggestion of a semicircular apse. The chancel would seem to have been a rectangular porticus, but it may yet turn out that from the middle part of the east wall there was a small semicircular projection. The nave is 38 ft. 4 in. long and

25 ft. wide; the original chancel was 20 ft. by 14 ft. 4 in.[1] At Monkwearmouth, built in 673 by Gallic masons in the Roman manner, the proportions are more regular, as are those of most of the very early churches in England which I have been able to examine. The remaining porticus at Monkwearmouth is 11 ft. 4 in. square, and the original nave was 22 ft. 8 in. broad and 68 ft. long, a very remarkable regularity of proportion [2].

So things went on, until at length the king declared that he was willing to become a Christian, and he was baptized. We may be sure that some great day of the Church's year would be chosen for this crowning event if any great day was fairly near at hand. The earliest tradition we have, and there is no counter tradition, entirely satisfies us in this respect. It tells us that Whitsunday—which may possibly have taken the earliest form of its Saxon name on this very account, at this very time—was the day chosen. No more suitable day could have been selected. In

---

[1] I should like strongly to recommend Canon Routledge's Monograph on *St. Martin's Church* (Kegan Paul & Co., 1891).

[2] *Notes on the original Church of St. Peter, Monkwearmouth*, with twelve illustrations, by G. F. Browne (Cambridge University Press, 1886).

1897, Pentecost falls on June 6, and on that day, no doubt, the thoughts of the English-speaking race in all parts of the world will be turned to Canterbury. We owe it to a successor of Augustine, Thomas a-Becket, that the octave of Pentecost was fixed in the English Church as the festival of the Holy Trinity, an example followed by Rome seven or eight generations later; and to this we owe our reckoning of the Sundays of the second half of the Christian year as "after Trinity." The English Church might well have kept to the reckoning from Pentecost, as Cambridge still lines the hoods of its Doctors of Divinity with silk shot with pink and violet, in imitation of the breast of the dove, because at Pentecost the power to confer that degree was given.

Where was Ethelbert baptized? How much that question has been discussed and debated! Bede does not tell us—and yet I think he does. The natural place, of course, was St. Martin's Church, to the modern mind. But, it has been objected, baptism was by immersion, and there is need of considerable space for that ceremony. Bede settles that question. In the church of St. Martin, he tells us, Augustine and his companions baptized. And, further, he tells us that they did so till after the conversion of the king. I do not see where there is room in those two statements for objection to the belief that the king's baptism took place in St. Martin's Church. Christian art shews us, by an abundance of early examples, that baptism by affusion was frequent; I think we might go further. At Ravenna there is more than one representation of baptism by affusion in mosaic work executed long before 597.

When we come to times later than Bede, tradition says distinctly that the baptism was at St. Martin's. Gocelin [1], in the eleventh century, gives vague details, which may perhaps be interpreted in two opposite senses:—"the church" (he can only mean St. Martin's at that date, I think) "is ornamented; the baptisteries are decorated; the urn of the river of Jordan and of Paradise is consecrated." John Bromton is the first, so far as Canon Routledge has ascertained, to say positively that the baptism of Ethelbert was at St. Martin's. He wrote a little before 1200.

The king, Bede tells us, was among those who were irresistibly attracted by the spot-

---

[1] *Acta Sanctorum*, May 26: sect. 22 of the Life of Augustine.

less life of the holy men, and by their most sweet and soothing promises. Their spotless life was manifest to all men; that their promises were true, there was the evidence of many miracles. So Bede says.

It is perfectly clear that Bede believed in the frequent exercise of miraculous power in the earlier times of the English Church. And it is equally clear that Augustine believed that he could himself exercise, and had exercised, such power. And, again, it is perfectly clear that Gregory accepted, as beyond question true, the information he received of the working of miracles by Augustine. We have a most interesting letter[1] which he wrote to Augustine on receiving the news. It is one of the letters which throw light on Augustine's character. Gregory warns him very solemnly against any feeling of self-satisfaction. He is to rejoice in fear, and to fear greatly in rejoicing. When God works by him external signs, he is always to subject himself to a close and subtle inward inquiry; to understand who and what he is, and how great grace there must be in the English people, that for their conversion even the gift of working wonders was bestowed upon him.

[1] *Ep.* xi. 28.

At such times he must recall to memory any offences he has ever committed, by word or deed, and so keep down the rising sense of personal glory. And he must remember that the gift is not given to him, but to those for whose salvation it is exercised.

Some fifteen years ago I had to publish an opinion on the miraculous stories related by Bede. Nothing which I have read since, or been able to think, on the subject, has tended to alter the opinion then expressed. It ran as follows:—

"On a review of Bede's writings as a whole, we may fairly say that the miraculous influence, claimed for illustrious missionaries, was confined to the first and second generation of Christian teachers in the land [1]. To say that even in the first and second generation there was no such influence at work, would be to say more than we are entitled to say. In the earliest years of a mission, as the experience of times later than those of Bede has shewn, there are occasions on which it is very difficult to say whether the divine power, which the Christian believes to be really working, has wrought openly; whether the Lord has,

[1] That is, in each separate missionary enterprise in a kingdom of the Heptarchy.

in fact, in the sight of men, confirmed the words of His apostles with signs following [1]."

The king had originally assigned to the mission an abode within the city. The early tradition of the place tells us that this was near the Stable Gate, so called because the pack-horses used to be put up there, in the present parish of St. Alphege. They were now to move to more important quarters. The king gave them a place of residence suitable to their position, in his capital city, and such other things of various kinds as were necessary for carrying on their work.

Gregory, as we know, had intended that if the English people received Augustine, he should be consecrated as their bishop. And he had arranged how this was to be done. He was to be consecrated by the German bishops, as he informs Eulogius in a letter [2] already quoted. By this he meant the Frankish bishops in possession of the Gallican sees. We might have expected that he would require Augustine to proceed to Rome for consecration. The journey was long, but it could not be said to be too long; for when the consecration was over, Augustine sent Laurentius,

---

[1] *The Venerable Bede*, S.P.C.K., 2nd ed., p. 171.
[2] *Ep.* viii. 30.

the most important man of his mission, to Rome, to inform the pope of the fact. It seems to me clear at every point that Gregory wished the English Church to feel and to be as free as Church could possibly be. The first consecration was the most important of all. Then, if ever, Gregory would make it clear beyond dispute that the whole thing hung upon the will of Rome. Whatever might be done in the case of later consecrations, this beginning of the Anglican succession must owe itself direct to Rome. But it was not so. Augustine went for consecration to the bishop of a Gallican see. He went to Ætherius, bishop of Arles, or Vergilius, there is some confusion of name or place, and by him was consecrated "archbishop for the English race," to quote Bede's phrase.

Gregory's statement to Augustine with regard to Arles, after his consecration, was this: ' We give you no authority among the bishops of Gaul, for from the ancient times of my predecessors the bishop of Arles has received the pallium, and we certainly must not deprive him of the authority he has received.' That Arles, in the extreme south of France, should come to be the ecclesiastical centre to which Augustine went for consecration to his

Kentish bishopric, is a curious and instructive fact of ancient history. It was enough to make more than one pope turn in his grave. Arles and Vienne had striven for the mastery, each contending that it was the metropolitan see of the province known as Gallia Narbonnensis. Pope Zosimus, the same who revoked his own decision in favour of Pelagius in a letter which stated that no one could question the pope's decision, had decreed in 417-8, in favour of Patroclus, bishop of Arles, that Arles should be the metropolitan see. He based this on a hardy statement that Trophimus the Ephesian was sent from Rome by St. Peter to found the Church of Arles; that he was the first metropolitan of the south of France; that such had always been the privilege of Arles; and that all were in consequence bound to respect that institution of primitive times. Of course the whole story of Trophimus the Ephesian was an invention, but that was the pope's statement. And he declared that Vienne and the whole of Gallia Narbonnensis, now subdivided into a First and a Second Narbonne, should be subject to the bishop or archbishop of Arles.

The bishop of Arles acted upon this, two years later, filling up a vacant bishopric.

Hilary, bishop of Narbonne, thereupon complained to the successor of Zosimus, Boniface I. This was the pope who had such a severe strife with an anti-pope, Eulalius, that the Emperor Honorius published an edict to the effect that if ever again two rival popes were elected, neither should be pope, and a new election must be made. What a confusion worse confounded this edict would have made, if it had been obeyed in the case of the fifty popes and anti-popes who at various times between that date and the year 1449 claimed in pairs, sometimes three at a time, to be the sole head of the Church, the sole voice of St. Peter speaking to the world, the sole voice of Christ speaking in St. Peter.

Boniface exactly contradicted his predecessor. He declared that the bishop of Arles must not exercise metropolitan authority, and bade the bishop of Narbonne act in that capacity. And the next pope, Celestine, reasserted this nine years after, about A.D. 428. Arles, however, appears to have continued to act as a metropolitan, in spite of popes' decrees.

About A.D. 444 the great Hilary, bishop of Arles, ordained bishops for Vienne. He also deposed a bishop; and, direst offence of all, he actually went so far as to speak slightly of the authority of St. Peter, and of the pope's supremacy. The deposed bishop appealed to Rome. Pope Leo decreed that Hilary must lose all his metropolitan rights, which must be transferred to Vienne; and he restored the deposed bishop. Leo was bound to say something about the decree of Zosimus in favour of Arles, which I have described above; so he remarked that the privilege appeared to have been given to Patroclus of Arles as a temporary measure, none of his predecessors having enjoyed it. How in the world that is to be reconciled with the decree of Zosimus, that Trophimus was sent by St. Peter to found the Church of Arles, that he was the first metropolitan, and that such had always been the privilege of Arles, the pope only knows.

The course of events does not so far promise to lead to the result that Augustine went to Arles to be consecrated, and was told by Gregory that from ancient times Arles had had the pallium. But Leo very soon indeed made yet another change of front. After Hilary's death, his successor and the clergy of the province petitioned Leo, in 450, for the restoration of the ancient metropolitan dignity which Arles had inherited from Trophimus.

Leo was pledged to the hilt to the declaration that neither Trophimus nor any bishop of Arles before 417 had possessed this privilege. But he proceeded to decree that what Hilary, the previous bishop, had deservedly lost by his presumption, might now be restored. He gave to Arles the metropolitan jurisdiction over the province, except that he made the bishop of Vienne metropolitan over Vienne and four neighbouring cities, on the ground that Vienne too was an ancient and honourable Church. Such were the contradictory decrees of fallible supremacy, which brought it about that Arles was the more important metropolis of the south of France. Why Augustine should have gone so far, when there were provinces of Gaul close at hand for him to go to, is not quite clear. Wilfrid in his time went to Paris, and the pope of his time supported him.

I have said that we might have supposed that Gregory would desire to consecrate Augustine himself. If it had been his intention to fasten a yoke upon the neck of the bishops of the English people, he would presumably have summoned him to Rome. The journey, as I have remarked, was long. But later popes told later archbishops of Canterbury that the length of the journey was no sufficient reason for their declining to come to Rome; and later archbishops did not always listen to that retort. Besides, after all, Augustine had to go down to the very south of France to be consecrated, and that was much more than half-way to Rome. He had himself afforded a sufficient argument against the plea that the passage of the mountains was too great a labour, by making that passage most unnecessarily, when he and his party turned back in fear from the supposed perils of a journey through France.

Gregory, however, in pursuance of his enlightened policy towards the beginning of a thoroughly national Church of England, though he may naturally have formed the wish, made no such demand. And Gregory was by no means alone in this policy. With the exception of Archbishop Theodore, in whose case the kings of Northumbria and Kent agreed to request the pope to find and consecrate an archbishop, the succession in England having practically come very near to an end, there is no record of an archbishop of Canterbury being consecrated out of England for 557 years. And even Theodore did not go out of England to be consecrated; he was living in Rome when he was selected for the archbishopric, and was consecrated there to be ready for his work as soon as he should arrive in England. Besides, there was at the time certainly not more than one bishop in England who could have been asked to perform the ceremony. All the great Norman archbishops — Lanfranc, Anselm, Theobald, Becket—were consecrated at Canterbury, by English bishops, Theobald being the only one with a direct foreign strain in his succession, Alberic, bishop of Ostia, who was then living as legate in England, with the English bishops, being his consecrators. The facts and dates of the foreign consecrations are an instructive lesson as to the period of the encroachments of Rome. Richard was consecrated at Anagni by Pope Alexander III in 1174; Stephen Langton at Viterbo by Pope Innocent III [1] in 1207; Boniface of Savoy at Lyons by Pope Innocent IV [1] in 1245, Edmund Rich having in the interval been consecrated at Canterbury in 1234 by eleven English and Irish bishops; and John Peckham at Rome by Pope Nicholas III in 1279, Robert Kilwardby having been consecrated at Canterbury in 1273 by thirteen English bishops. When John Peckham had

[1] Popes Innocent III and IV each consecrated at various dates three others of the English bishops.

received consecration from the pope, the bill was presented to him. It came to 5,000 marks, say £50,000 at least, of present money. He was aghast, for he was a mendicant. He described it as "horribilis in aspectu, et auditu terribilis," horrible even to look at, and when the items and the amounts were read, frightful. It is rather comical that never again was an archbishop of Canterbury consecrated by a pope. Three more received consecration abroad, at the hands of Roman cardinals, at Aquileia and Avignon, in 1294, 1328, and 1349. Later in the year 1349 Simon Islip was consecrated archbishop in St. Paul's by three English bishops, and thenceforward such of our archbishops of Canterbury as were not translated from other sees were consecrated at home by English bishops. It is well to bear in mind, in order that we may see the significance of all this, that 1174, when it began, was well on in the reign of Henry II, and that 1349, when it came to an end, was just the date at which the English rulers and the English people had become thoroughly sick of the ridiculous extortions of Rome. In 1350 the great Act against Provisions was passed, and in 1353 the great Act called Praemunire; and in 1367, on the king informing Parliament that even these Acts had not brought the remedy that had been expected, Parliament determined that the Pope must be resisted with all the power of the realm. That was 160 years before Henry VIII saw Anne Boleyn.

I have said that such of the archbishops of Canterbury as were not translated from other sees were from 1349 onwards consecrated at home. Of those who were translated from other sees, only one, Henry Chicheley, was consecrated bishop by a pope. He was consecrated bishop of St. David's by Pope [1] Gregory XII at Lucca in 1408, and translated to Canterbury in 1414. That same year, 1414, saw the last consecration of an English bishop by a pope, that of the next bishop of St. David's, John Catterick, who was consecrated at Bologna by Pope John XXIII. Again the date is most instructive. That year, 1414, heralded the final end. The knell of the popes had begun to ring. The Council of Constance met the very next year, with the avowed purpose of reforming the terrible abuses of the Papacy. Their idea of reform was a fairly sweeping one, and indeed it was time, for there were three popes, each claiming

[1] Pope or Anti-pope, who shall say?

to be the one only pope, each—may we so put it—nearly as bad as the other two. They tried this same Pope John XXIII on fifty-six charges, fourteen of the original seventy having been withdrawn because they were too vile to be read in public; they condemned him, deposed him, and had another pope elected in his stead. It is a quaint fact that he was the last pope who ever consecrated a bishop for the English Church. And that, though 120 years had still to pass before England took the last of its long series of steps to put an end to the encroachments of Rome; encroachments which were comparatively quite modern, and found no precedent or encouragement in any act or word of Pope Gregory, whom we rightly call the Great.

In this connection of the independence of the English Episcopate from the earliest times, as shadowed forth in the consecration of Augustine, the complaint of Pope Paschal in 1115 is much in point. The English bishops bound themselves to complete obedience to their metropolitan, reserving no obedience to the pope. It is quite in accordance with the earliest facts. That it was in accordance with the facts of Paschal's time is one of the most valuable testimonies to our independence that could have been given. It is worthy to be compared with the confession of Pope Honorius, in 1225, that justice was openly sold in Rome or made unnecessarily expensive; the remedy he suggested being that he should be rescued from the poverty, which made this necessary, by the gift of two prebends in each cathedral and abbey in England. We are told, and it does not surprise us, that this proposal made the great council of the nation roar with laughter, when it was read to them by the archbishop.

The earliest extant profession of obedience of an English bishop to the Archbishop of Canterbury dates in 796. It is specially in point, because events then recent rendered it specially necessary to emphasise the position of Canterbury, the metropolitical see having been some years before removed to Lichfield. It had now been brought back to Canterbury. This causes the introduction of Pope Gregory's name, so that Rome is not passed over *sub silentio*, as was usually the case with us then. The bishop pledges himself, so long as he shall live, 'always to be careful to submit the neck of his humble obedience to Ethelheard the Archbishop of Canterbury and his successors. For it is right that he and all his fellow bishops look to the episcopal see of the blessed Augustine, to the City of Canterbury, whence is ministered to all of them the order of ecclesiastical dignity, as the blessed Gregory directed.' As a fact, Gregory had directed that London, not Canterbury, should be the metropolis of the south, but that has nothing to do with this declaration of obedience. This is the only reference I can find in these "professions" to the controversy between Canterbury and Lichfield, but in other respects the document is followed with ever-varying phrase by all like documents for hundreds of years. Anything more unlike dependence upon Rome it would be difficult to invent.

I may as well, having said so much on considerations rising directly out of the consecration of the first bishop and archbishop of the English, say a few words on the earliest synodical enactment respecting appeals. In or about 747, the Englishman who had been the apostle of Germany, that is, Boniface the Archbishop of Mainz, wrote to Cuthbert his friend, the Archbishop of Canterbury, that at a German synod they had resolved that "if any bishop found in his diocese matters which he was unable to correct and amend, he should bring them before the archbishop in full synod with a view to their being corrected. And this in the same manner as the Roman Church bound with an oath those whom it ordained, that if they were unable to correct priests or people they should take the matter always to the apostolic see and the Vicar of St. Peter for amendment; for thus all bishops were "— in the opinion of Boniface—"bound to act towards their metropolitan, and he towards the Roman Pontiff[1]." It is a difficult question whether this letter preceded the English Council of Cloveshoo or followed it. In either case, the fact remains, that the Council of Cloveshoo enacted the first part, directing bishops to bring matters which were too difficult for them to the archbishop in full synod to be corrected. There they stopped. The archbishop was the final appeal. They did not enact the second part, directing the metropolitan to bring matters which were too difficult for him to the apostolic see and the Vicar of St. Peter. The significance of this cannot be overrated. Boniface did all he could to bring the English Church to take the view he had persuaded the German Church to take, and he failed entirely.

[1] Haddan and Stubbs, iii. 371, 378.

I remarked, at an earlier point, that if Gregory had intended to fasten the yoke of Rome upon us, he would have made his intention clear. And this was especially necessary, considering the character of the man with whom he had to deal here, Augustine. Some of his letters to Augustine remind us of the patience with which a good teacher in a Sunday school gets ideas into the heads of the upper classes in the school; partly by persuading them that they already know what is being taught them, partly by putting the ideas into language of a very simple kind. We can imagine that behind the scenes Gregory was just a little cross with this correspondent of his, just a little impatient that he seemed so little able to go alone. Ability to go alone was perhaps not quite the quality that the popes of the later Middle Ages looked for; but then they were not men like Gregory, desiring to intervene as little as possible. They desired to exercise dominion, lordship, and the greater the number of points referred to them, the better they were pleased. Of this spirit, of this desire, we see in Gregory no sign at all. Nay, the signs are all the other way. In this as in some other respects, as for instance his rejection of the title "universal bishop," it is not too much to say that if Gregory had foreseen the ridiculous and mischievous claims of his successors, and had desired to do what he could to neutralise them, he could scarcely have acted with greater care and prudence than he did in his relations with England.

The fact is that we shall never estimate aright the attitude of Gregory to the Church of England, if we have not realised the vast difference there was between his position and the position of the mediaeval popes. His predecessors had seen the see of Rome fall very low, partly from their own fault, partly from the force of circumstances. There probably has never been a sadder time for the Papacy, if we except the abnormal vileness of the period of the Hetaerocracy, a period that clamours for exception when men are speaking of laws human or divine, of the chastity of women or the decency of men, above all when men are speaking of those who called themselves vicars of Christ on earth. Except in that time of exceptional evil, and except in the time of the popes of Henry VIII's earlier years, there has probably not been a sadder time for the Papacy than the years which saw the degradation of Pope Silverius, and the session of Pope Vigilius, the creature of the Empress Theodora. Between that time and Gregory there were only three insignificant bishops of Rome. He had to build up in all directions. The reputation of his see, the services of the Church, the property of the poor, all had to be organised and set going as it were afresh. Political affairs of the most pressing kind demanded his attention, practically as though he were the sovereign of the City of Rome, a city sunk so low, the prey of this and the other barbarian. The Donation of Constantine had not as yet been forged, was not forged probably for some 150 years after his time, so that there was no foolish question of any ownership of England by the popes. Britain had long ago been severed from the western empire, and left to fend for itself, almost immediately after the final division of the empire into east and west. The western empire itself had now come to an end, had been out of existence for more than a hundred years. And Gregory clearly had no idea of reviving any arrangement based upon the western empire in times when Britain was under a Roman governor as part of the province of the Gauls. Ecclesiastical England was to be clear of all the ties that had bound secular Britain, even if Gregory knew what those ties had been. Everything pointed to his leaving our Church as much as possible to manage its own affairs under Augustine; and so for the few brief years from 597, when they founded it, to 604, when they both died, so he did leave it. Alas that later follies have made these polemical digressions necessary.

Augustine had acted, in the matter of his consecration, without making, so far as we know, any communication to Gregory. As soon as the consecration was completed, he sent the priest Laurentius, who soon after became his successor, and Peter the monk, who became abbat of the second monastery, to inform the pope that the English had accepted the faith of Christ, and that he had himself been made bishop. At the same time he sent to Gregory a number of questions which had puzzled him in connection with the converts from paganism; and to these Gregory sent written answers. We have the whole complete [1], but I shall only touch on those which specially concern our history.

Augustine asks:—"The faith being one, why are there diversities of custom between

[1] Bede, i. 29.

one Church and another? Why is one custom of masses observed in the holy Roman Church and another in the Church of the Gallic provinces?"

Gregory replies:—"My brother knows the custom of the Roman Church, in which he remembers that he was brought up. But my pleasure is, that you should with great care select whatever you think will best please Almighty God, wherever you find it, whether in the Church of Rome, or in the Church of Gaul, or in any other Church. And then plant firmly in the Church of the English that which you have collected in many Churches. For things are not to be loved because of places, but places because of things in them that are good."

On this admirably broad conception of the course to be pursued, I will only remark that if Gregory had desired to declare, in set terms, that which we hold of the independence of national Churches, and their freedom to determine rites and ceremonies, and manage their own most important affairs, he could not well have done it in clearer words. He takes the central point of all, the manner and words of celebrating the Holy Eucharist, and even there he declares that the Church of the English is to have its own independent uses, uses which may be derived from Churches other than the Church of Rome.

Augustine asks:—" Within what degree of relationship may people marry?"

Gregory replies:—" The secular Roman law allows first cousins to marry; but we forbid it absolutely; they must by all means abstain from one another. None nearer than second cousins can be married lawfully. Further, a man may not marry his sister-in-law, for by the former marriage she became his brother's flesh. Two brothers may lawfully marry two sisters."

Gregory got rather into a scrape about this answer. It is a curious example of the rapidity with which news spread in those days. Felix, bishop of Messana, who was brought up in Rome, and reminded Gregory that he had taught Augustine, wrote to express his surprise that Gregory had widely departed from the Roman rule with regard to consanguinity. Gregory replied that he had made concessions to the new converts, lest they should be deterred from becoming Christians by the severity of the conditions which governed the relation between the sexes. When they were firmly fixed in the faith, persons found married within the seventh generation must be separated[1]. The whole city of Rome was his witness that this was the intention with which he wrote. He solemnly called God to witness that nothing else was in his mind.

Augustine asks :—"If distances are so great that bishops cannot easily come together, may a bishop be consecrated by one bishop alone?"

Gregory replies :—"As regards the Church of the English, in which you are so far the only bishop, you cannot ordain a bishop except in the absence of other bishops, unless some bishops came from the Gauls to assist as witnesses in the ordination of a bishop. But we wish you so to ordain bishops that they may not be very far apart; that when a bishop is to be ordained, bishops may come together, and the pastors also, whose presence is very useful. When things have been got into full order, there must be no ordination of a bishop unless three or four bishops are present."

Here again Gregory shews an independence of judgment and action which goes far beyond the ordinary limits. The voice of

---

[1] Innocent III relaxed this rule, and permitted marriage after the fourth degree; that is, fourth cousins might marry, third cousins might not.

catholic antiquity pronounced that there ought to be three bishops present. To carry this question into its issues would transgress our bounds of subject and of time.

Augustine asks:—" How are we to deal with the bishops of the provinces of Gaul and the British Isles [1]?"

Gregory replies:—" From the ancient times of my predecessors, the bishop of Arles has received the pallium [2]; we must by no means deprive him of the authority he has received; we give you no authority among the Gallican bishops. All the bishops of the British Isles [3] we commit to you, my brother, that those who are unlearned may be taught, the weak may be strengthened by persuasion, the perverse corrected by authority."

This is the first mention we have had of the bishops of the British Church. It seems probable that the existence of the British Church had been lost sight of, and that Laurentius and Peter informed Gregory on

---

[1] Galliarum Britaniarumque. Galliae, "the Gauls," can only be without ambiguity rendered as in the text. Britaniae might in earlier times have meant the provinces of Britain, but I suppose the text is a fair expression of the meaning here.

[2] See p. 60.

[3] Still Britaniarum.

the subject by word of mouth. Gregory's decision cannot have been arrived at on full knowledge, or on any sufficiently exhaustive enquiry, and it savours of haste and want of statesmanship. The point was one of much greater importance than they imagined, both practically and in catholic principle. A little more care at this crisis might have produced effects permanently good; whereas the harm actually done was great[1]. This mistake of Gregory's seems to me not only relatively the greatest defect in his usually wise decisions, but also in itself an error very great and serious.

After his consecration success continued to attend upon Augustine's efforts. He reported to Gregory that he found himself short of men, so great had the work become. Gregory tells Eulogius of Alexandria a fact which we do not learn from Bede, that no less than ten thousand of the English were baptized on Christmas Day. An early tradition tells that this multitudinous baptism took place in the river Swale; and as the Swale is a well-known river in the north, forming with the Ure the Yorkshire Ouse, the mediaeval chroniclers and writers of lives had to take Augustine up into

[1] See pp. 107, 108.

Northumbria, and to invent the details of his preaching and baptizing there. This they did very thoroughly while they were about it. But, in fact, the Swale is also the name of the river which separates the Isle of Sheppey from Kent, and runs into the sea on the coast of Kent, at Whitstable Bay. This is one among many examples where a little local knowledge would have saved writers from grave blunders.

In response to Augustine's request for more men, Gregory sent a very important addition to the staff, the principal personages of this second band of missionaries being Mellitus, Justus, Paulinus, and Rufinianus. Two of these became archbishops of Canterbury, and one archbishop of York: Rufinianus became abbat. With the new missionaries he sent all things needed for the worship and ministry of the Church, sacred vessels and vestments for the altars, ornaments of the churches, robes for the priests and clerks, relics of the holy apostles and martyrs, and a large number of books.

We have the Canterbury list of such of these books as were still in existence at Canterbury in the year 1300. There was a great Bible in two volumes, called the Bible of Gregory: at the beginning of each of the books in it were coloured sheets of vellum, some purple, some rose-colour. These noble volumes were still known in 1604. Of the six remaining books of the list, I will only mention here two. One was the book of the Gospels known as St. Mildred's, because a man in the Isle of Thanet swore a false oath upon it and became blind; this book is believed now to be in the Bodleian Library. The other was also a book of the Gospels; it is believed to be in the Library of Corpus Christi College, Cambridge, and a very beautiful book it is, certainly a book of Gregory's time. Of the personal vestments, six copes and a chasuble remained in 1300, and the moderation of the claim, both here and in the list of books, is in its favour. All were of silk. One cope was of sapphire or azure colour, with borders of gold, adorned in front, in the upper part, with stones. Two were of purple; in other respects like that just mentioned. Three were also of purple silk, but they were inwoven in every part with threads of gold and milk-coloured silk, in another part described as snow-white. The chasuble was purple, adorned in front, at the upper part, with stones. The writer of the list points out that the number of copes corresponded with the number of those who brought them, Laurentius and Peter, Augustine's messengers, and Mellitus, Justus, Paulinus, and Rufinianus, sent by Gregory. Of the sacred vessels the writer grieves that he can give no account. One story was that they were hid in the time of the Danish invasions, and no one knew where they had been put; another that they were sold to help towards the ransom of King Richard. Let us hope the first was the true story, for then they may possibly still be found.

At the same time, that is on June 22, 601, Gregory wrote to Augustine a letter which he clearly intended to be the Charter of the English Church[1]. Every sentence in it is of importance. It should be explained that Gregory's plan was that Canterbury should give place to London at Augustine's death, a plan which was not carried out.

The letter runs thus:—

"To his most reverend and most holy brother Augustine his fellow bishop, Gregory the servant of the servants of God.

"While it is certain that ineffable rewards of the eternal kingdom are reserved for those who labour for the omnipotent God, it is still incumbent on us to bestow honours upon

---

[1] Bede, i. 29.

them, that by this reward they may be strengthened to labour more than ever in their spiritual work. And since the new Church of the English has been brought to the grace of God by thy labours, the same Lord giving His favour, we concede to thee the use of the pallium in the said Church of the English, but only for the celebration of masses: so that thou mayest ordain twelve bishops subject to thy authority, in various places; with this understanding, that for the future the bishop of London city must always be consecrated by his own synod, and receive the pallium of honour from this holy and apostolic Church which I by the will of God serve. To York city we will that thou send a bishop, whom thou shalt choose to ordain, so that if that city and the neighbouring district receive the word of God, he also may ordain twelve bishops and enjoy the honour of a metropolitan; for on him also we propose to bestow the pallium, if life last and the Lord will. We will that he be subject to thee; but after thy death he shall so rule the bishops whom he has ordained, as to be under no subjection to the bishop of London. And for the future let there be this distinction of honour between the bishops of the city of London and of York, that he have precedence who was first ordained. But let them with common counsel and concordant action arrange with one mind such things as are to be done for zeal of Christ; let them come to right conclusions, and carry them out without differences. Thou, my brother, must have under thine authority, God our Lord Jesus Christ so willing, not only the bishops whom thou hast ordained, nor those only who have been ordained by the bishop of York, but also all the priests (or bishops[1]) of Britain, that from thy holy speech and life they may receive the rule of right belief and of well living.

"God keep thee safe, most reverend brother."

When we look into these careful regulations, we see, first of all, that Gregory intended the

---

[1] *Sacerdotes.* The word hitherto invariably used by Gregory has been *episcopus.* In his letter to the Frank kings, he says that requests had come from England to the *sacerdotes* of the neighbourhood, and advises that *presbyteri* be sent with Augustine. There appears to be considerable uncertainty as to the dates at which *sacerdotes* may be taken to mean, or to include, bishops. The question is raised by two of the many interesting memorials of early times in this island, *sancti et praecipui sacerdotes* on a British stone at Kirkmadrine in Galloway, and *Trumberect Sac* on an Anglian stone from Yarm, now at Durham. See p. 155; and, also, pp. 156, 7.

episcopal succession in the Church of the English to be kept up by and in the English Church. The metropolitans are to consecrate the bishops, when once Augustine has consecrated the metropolitans and has set going the province of the south. The case of a vacancy in the metropolitical see of the south is arranged for; the synod of the south is to fill the vacancy. Not a word is said of any permission from Rome. And yet, such have been the encroachments of Rome since that time, that a modern controversialist has said that after Pole there has been no archbishop of Canterbury, because the pope never gave permission for the consecration of a successor to Pole, and has never given permission since. But the consecration of Archbishop Parker was in accordance with Gregory's charter. Gregory's mind was large and broad, and his regulations for us were reasonable and free.

The case of a vacancy in the metropolitical see of the north, Gregory does not deal with. The same rule would naturally prevail as in the south. Here, as in the case of London (that is, Canterbury), there is not the faintest hint of any reference to any external person, except so far as this, that the pallium was promised by Gregory. There is no hint that to withhold the pallium will stop the succession. The law of succession is to be self-working.

Our arrangements for keeping up the episcopal succession are in accordance with the principles laid down by Gregory for the permanent guidance of the new Church—its guidance for the future, as he more than once emphatically says. If an archbishopric is vacant, a commission is issued, to the other archbishop and two bishops, or to four bishops, to consecrate an archbishop in his place, if the person chosen is not already a bishop. If a bishopric is vacant, a commission is issued to the archbishop of the province, if the archbishopric be not void, and to the other archbishop if it be void, to proceed to consecrate a bishop to the vacant bishopric. It would appear from the Act (25 Hen. VIII. c. 20) that a bishopric cannot be filled during a vacancy in both archbishoprics. One of the archbishoprics must first be filled. The whole arrangements of the Act made it clear that those who drew it had full knowledge of, and complete respect for, catholic antiquity and catholic principle. The minimum number of consecrators is ascertained from the Act relating to suffragans, where it is required that two other bishops or suffragans shall consecrate the new suffragan with the archbishop. The wording of this enactment declares the mind of the most learned men of Henry VIII's time on one very important question, and men more learned there certainly were not elsewhere ; namely, that the assistant bishops are consecrators, as well as the chief bishop. See p. 192.

The mention of the pallium in this letter is of the highest importance ; for the pallium was, more than anything else, the material by which the popes built up their claims upon metropolitans. It was in itself the survival of an imperial robe, which Byzantine emperors had allowed great ecclesiastics to wear, and others whom they wished to honour, without incurring the penalty of high treason which attended the wearing of an imperial robe. Then the bishops of Rome were allowed to grant the use of it to those whom they in turn desired to honour, in cases approved by the emperor. Later, the bishops of Rome granted it to whom they would, not to metropolitans only. It had come to be a strip of white wool, twisted round the neck, with one end hanging down in front and the other behind. It was ornamented with crosses and fastened with pins. In the course of time the popes brought it about that the gift of the pall was regarded as the seal of metropolitical authority, so that if a pope refused to grant the pall to an archbishop, he deprived the archbishop of the power to act as a metropolitan. That was the point to which the claim at last reached, and on a more flimsy basis surely never was a claim so enormous founded, a claim to power so destructive. This is one of the cases in which the exercise of the powers claimed by later popes would, if recognised as lawful, throw into hopeless confusion the apostolical succession.

But in this letter Gregory appears to say that the gift of the pall shall as a matter of course follow upon the consecration of the metropolitan bishop of London. And as regards York, the bishop is to enjoy the honour of a metropolitan; that is settled: if Gregory lives, he proposes to send to him too the pall; if he should not live, still, so it appears, York would be a metropolitan. That is one of two opposite views of the meaning as regards York, and only as such do I give it. I am myself satisfied to say, that the origin of the use of the pall was of such a nature, that if, in the sixteenth century, a bishop of Rome chose to withhold the pall from the spiritual head of a national Church, the national Church had a perfect right to throw itself back upon the foundations of the Christian faith and practice. We can say, "We go on in confidence without it. If the pall is vitally necessary to the existence of a Church, it must always have been necessary. You cannot invent after a thousand years a new vital necessity. If we are not a Church because you please not to give us the pall, then there is no Church anywhere; for there were centuries of the existence of the Church when the pall had not been heard of, even as an ecclesiastical dress, much less as a badge of metropolitical power." For more on this point see p. 192.

The records of England and of Rome have more than one comical story about the pall, due to the unfortunate habit Rome had of giving to the world of the west more than one sole pope at a time. Poor Stigand went to the only pope then acting, to get his pall, and at the end of his life the pope's people deposed him for having got the pall from an antipope, though no other pope was acting at the time, and the acts of the pope he got it from were never annulled.

Again, Gregory speaks of the Church here as a "new Church," "the new Church of the English." He has spoken in his previous letter of "the Church of the Gallic provinces." To say, as some modern controversialists are hardy enough to say, that both were "Roman Catholic Churches," is to forge history. Romans have precedents enough in their own records for that process; but it is out of date now. From Gregory's first establishment of a Church among the Anglo-Saxons, it was *Ecclesia Anglorum*, the Church of the English. And in the preamble of the great Act of Supremacy (26 Hen. VIII. cap. 1) it was so still, as it has ever been; "the Church of England, called *Anglicana Ecclesia.*" It was so in Magna Charta, the Charter of the liberties of Englishmen, which the pope of course cursed with all his might and main. The national assertion of liberty was naturally met in that spirit by Rome.

It is a very remarkable fact that not once in all the letters of Gregory preserved by Bede does he mention Rome or claim to be the successor of St. Peter. He once mentions the Roman Church, when a question of Augustine's forces him to do so; but he only mentions it then side by side with others;

"the Roman Church," he says, "the Gallican Church, and any other Church." And he mentions it only to say expressly that the English Church was not to be bound to follow it even in the most solemn act of the Church, the celebration of masses. And while Augustine's question calls it "the holy Roman Church," Gregory's reply calls it merely "the Roman Church." Time after time, on the other hand, he speaks of the Church of the English. Once he speaks of a Roman custom, and in a very instructive manner. "Different nations," he says in answer to Augustine's questions on a matter connected with marriage, "have different customs. The custom of the Romans has from ancient times been" so-and-so. That is a valuable indication of his view as to national customs. Again, once he speaks of the Church as a whole, "the Church" does so-and-so. He does not say "the Roman Church," or "the Holy Roman Church," but merely "Holy Church." Finally, once and once only does he mention St. Peter; and then it is only to say that though his presents to Ethelbert are small, they will not be small to him, being received from the benediction of the blessed Apostle Peter.

Look into the matter where you will, you

find a careful absence of everything that might have looked like a germ of the claims of later popes.

On the same day with this great letter to Augustine, Gregory dated a letter to King Ethelbert, "the most glorious lord and most excellent son."

"God Almighty sets good men to rule over nations, that through them He may bestow the gifts of His mercy. This He has done in the English nation, that blessings from on high may be theirs. Keep carefully that divine gift which you have received; hasten to spread the faith of Christ among those under your rule; multiply your zeal in their conversion; put down the worship of idols; overthrow their shrines [1]; build up the moral nature of your subjects by the great cleanness of your life; exhort, terrify, soothe, correct; shew them the example of good works: that you may find your rewarder in heaven.

"It was so that Constantine called the republic of Rome from its perverse worshippings of idols, and brought it and himself into subjection to Almighty God our Lord Jesus Christ; and his fame transcended the fame of the princes that had gone before.

[1] For more on this point, see p. 131.

"Our most reverend brother, Augustine the bishop, is fully instructed in monastic rule, is full of knowledge of Holy Scripture, and, by the grace of God, is endued with good works. Give ear to his admonitions, act upon them, keep them in your memory.

"We would have your glory know, that, as we gather from Holy Scripture and the words of Almighty God, the end of this present world is at hand, and the kingdom of Saints, which shall never end, is about to come. Before that time, many terrors shall appear in earth and air and sky. Let not these disturb your mind; they are signs, sent that men may prepare to meet the Judge.

"I send you some small presents. They will not seem small to you, for you receive them from the benediction of the blessed Peter the Apostle.

"May grace from on high keep your excellency safe, my lord son."

A dignified letter; worthy of Gregory and of Ethelbert.

LECTURE III.

A cathedral church built.—First conference with the Britons. — Welsh monasteries and bishoprics. — Second conference; failure.—Bishoprics of London and Rochester. —Endowments.—Death of Augustine.—Dedications of churches; St. Martin, Christ Church, St. John Baptist, St. Peter and St. Paul (St. Pancras), St. Mary, St. Andrew, St. Paul.

AUGUSTINE'S own position in England having now been defined, and a complete future sketched for the national Church of England, rapid progress was made in Canterbury. A cathedral church was built, with residences for the monks who formed its chapter. An abbey church, also, was commenced, for another set of monks; but it was not completed or consecrated in Augustine's time. All these matters of church building and dedication I propose to group together in the later part of this lecture. For the present I pass them by, and proceed with the personal narrative.

It was not for nothing that Augustine had been made supreme, so far as Gregory could make him supreme, over all the bishops of the provinces of Britain. He determined to act on his new power. The Britons in Wales were under no subjection to Ethelbert, or to any other of the Saxon kings. And though Ethelbert's overlordship was recognised from the south coast to the Humber, it did not reach westward, in these southern parts, further than the west border of the Middle Saxons. The whole of the West-Saxon territory lay between Augustine and the Britons in Wales. Ethelbert, however, was a powerful man, with wide influence; and Augustine made use of his good offices with the West Saxons, and sent through their land a message to the British bishops. He invited to a conference with him "the bishops or doctors of the nearest province of the Britons," at a place which was called in Bede's time, in the English tongue, *Augustinœs Ac*, Augustine's Oak.

Where this place was has been a matter of dispute. Many places claim the honour. Every one would wish to know, if it were possible, just where it was that the tall, gaunt, self-satisfied man from Italy met the thickset self-satisfied men from Wales. Bede gives us a clear line upon which we must set the oak thus made famous. I need not stop to remind you how, time after time, we have illustrations of the fact in our early history that a great conspicuous tree, not of any very great height perhaps, but spreading its thick-leaved branches far and wide, was recognised as a regular trysting place. Under the shadow of such a tree no doubt it was arranged that the conference should take place. "On the border of the Hwiccas and the West Saxons," Bede says, and that border-line is well known. The Hwiccas occupied Gloucestershire, Worcestershire, and the southern part of Warwickshire; the West Saxons marched with them all along their eastern border. Thus the conference took place somewhere on the eastern border of Gloucestershire, Worcestershire, and Warwickshire. Looking at the lie of the Roman roads, it seems to me practically certain that if you draw a line between Swindon in Wessex and Cirencester in Gloucestershire, the point where that line cuts the county boundary is as near as may be to Augustine's Oak. It cuts it at Cricklade. The Thames, as it seems to me, and not the Severn, is the river to be looked to, unless we are quite to disregard both Bede's words and the facts of physical geography as emphasised by the Roman road-makers. I am only too well aware of the commanding importance of the authorities from whom I differ in this calculation, and of the great weight which the name of Aust, at the Passage of the Severn, gives to their conclusions [1].

It is true that this puts the conference a long way from the borders of Wales. But that is one of the strongest arguments in its favour. Why should Augustine go the whole way from Kent to Wales, and not rather suggest a half-way house? The natural supposition is that the Welsh would be asked to come as far east as they could, without entering upon the territory of their enemies, the West Saxons. The Hwiccas, a Saxon people, were allied with the Welsh against the West Saxons; and through their territory the Welsh would feel no difficulty in travelling. As the crow flies, Cricklade is 130 miles from Canterbury. Disregarding the Bristol Channel, it is only 50 miles from Caerleon, 60 from Llandaff, 80 from Margam, 100 from Llanbadarn, 110 from Bangor under the wood, 130 from St. Asaph, and 150 from episcopal Bangor and from St. David's, supposing that St. David's

[1] Haddan and Stubbs, iii. 41.

was at that time the actual place of the bishop's abode. I cannot see why Augustine should be expected to go 50 miles further still from Canterbury. It is a coincidence, but nothing more, that a line drawn from Canterbury to St. David's passes about 4 miles south of Cricklade, and its middle point is about 9 miles west of that place.

I will not compare this synod of the Oak with that other synod of the Oak[1], held just 200 years before, which turned so much upon metropolitical jealousies and condemned Chrysostom. Augustine began by brotherly admonition to urge the Britons to make catholic peace with him. It was clear, then, that he regarded it as necessary that some formal action should be taken on their part to bring him and them, his Church and their Church, to be at one. That is, as things were, they were not at one. Ecclesiastical and formal unity having been secured, by whatever action might be necessary, they were then to take a joint interest in spreading the gospel among the heathen peoples. And here Bede interposes an explanation of the need for some action, to secure catholic peace. The Britons, he says, did not keep the Lord's Day of the

[1] A villa near Chalcedon, A.D. 403.

Passover at its proper time, but from the fourteenth to the twentieth of the moon, a reckoning contained in a cycle of eighty-four years; and very many other things they did contrary to ecclesiastical unity. On this I will only remark that Bede's phrase entirely acquits the Britons of the groundless charge made against them, that they were Quartodecimans, that is, kept Easter Day on the fourteenth of the moon, whether Sunday or week-day. He distinctly says that they did not take the same extreme limits for the incidence of Easter Sunday which he regarded as the proper limits. It was really a question of cycle; that is, of the number of years in which the sun, moon, and earth come back again to the same relative position. This is nearly true of nineteen years, which is one cycle; more nearly true of ninety-five, which is another.

The Britons held their own firmly. The disputation lasted long. What would we not give for ever so meagre a report of it; or such a report as we have of the debate in the Northumbrian House of Lords, or at the Conference of Whitby? The British firmness produced its natural effect upon men like Augustine. They began by praying the

Britons to take their view; they went on to exhorting them; they ended by scolding them. And not to any of these methods and tempers did the British give any heed. There was no King Oswi there, to bring them to agreement by a kindly joke about St. Peter shutting the gates of heaven in his face if he differed from him on this point. To the last they preferred their own traditions to all that they were told of the agreement of all the Churches in the world. Considering the state of some of those other Churches, they were probably told something a little beyond the facts.

This brings us to the last weapon in Augustine's armoury, scolding having been the last but one. I accept the story as given by Bede, but withhold an expression of opinion as to Augustine's part in it. Augustine proposed that some afflicted person should be brought before them, and each party should try to heal him by the efficacy of their prayers. The Britons consented, but unwillingly. A blind man was brought. The British priests did what they could, but they could do nothing. Then Augustine knelt down and prayed, and immediately the man received his sight. Thereupon the Britons confessed that Augustine's was the true way of righteousness. But, they said, they could not commit themselves to a change from their ancient customs, without the consent and permission of those whom they represented. They asked that a second conference should be held, when more of them would come. I must confess to a feeling of surprise that they took the defeat so meekly, considering, first, that they were Welshmen, and next, that the man experimented on was of English race. The modern representative of the Principality would have claimed to try with a Welshman.

The story goes, Bede says, that to this second conference there came no less than seven bishops of the Britons; to meet the one only bishop the English Church possessed. There came, also, many very learned men, chiefly from their most noble monastery called in English Bancornaburg, of which it was said that Dinoot was abbat. This, as we know, was not episcopal Bangor, but Bangor ys y Coed, Bangor under the Wood, 10 or 12 miles south of Chester; and the Dinoot of Bede is the Welsh Dunawd. Bede knew what a noble monastery was, and what a very learned man was, and we must take his superlative praise as meaning a great deal;

especially when we remember that the monastery of Llanyltud, now Llantwit Major in Glamorganshire, the home of David and of Gildas, was an older and more famous monastery still than Bangor; while, again, no college of the Britons had more famous pupils than Pawl Hen's college of Ty-gwyn ar Dâf, the white house on the Tave, now Whiteland in Carmarthenshire. It is a valuable illustration of the fact that the country we call Wales was recognised as a land of refuge for oppressed Britons, wherever they might be found, to know that all of these three really great seats of learning were founded by refugees. Iltyd came over from Brittany when princes and people were squeezed out by the advance of the Frankish arms; and Dunawd and Pawl Hen were North British chieftains, driven from their homes by reverses.

As we saw last year, there were at least six bishops' seats in Wales at the time of which we are speaking. In modern terms, they were St. David's, Llandaff, Llanbadarn Vawr, Bangor, St. Asaph (Llanelwy), Llanafan Vawr. To these it seems probable that we may add Margam in Glamorganshire, called then the bishopric of Morganwg. The Welsh traditions say that the Bishop of Hereford (Caerfawydd) was one of those present, and they omit St. David's; perhaps, as has been suggested, because a successor had not as yet been appointed to David himself, who probably died a year or two before the conference. Some, to make up the seven, have brought two British bishops up from Cornwall; others have suggested that there may have been in Wales, as at Iona and elsewhere, bishops in monasteries, as well as diocesan bishops.

Before the second conference, the British leaders consulted a holy and prudent man, who lived the anchoritic life among them, on this question, "Ought they, on the teaching of Augustine, to desert their own traditions?" I feel sure that we must credit them with putting the question in full earnest: it seems to me certain that their minds were open to adopt Augustine's practice, if they saw the way fairly clear. And the anchorite's answer is quite startlingly broad and bold—"If he is a man of God, follow him." "And how," they naturally asked, "are we able to test that?" He replied, "The Lord saith [1], 'Take My yoke upon you, and learn of Me, for I am meek and lowly in heart.' If, then, Augustine is meek and lowly in heart, you may believe that he

[1] St. Matt. xi. 29.

himself bears Christ's yoke, and that he offers it to you also to be borne. But if he is not meek, is proud, it is clear that he is not of God, nor need we regard his teaching." "And by what means," they asked, "are we to discern even this?" "Arrange beforehand," he advised them, "that he and his people arrive first at the place of the synod. If he rises to receive you when you approach, know that he is a servant of Christ, and hear him with willing attention. But if he spurns you, and does not choose to rise when you appear though you are more in number than he, let him in turn be spurned by you."

They acted on this advice. It turned out that when they came Augustine remained seated. They became angry, noting him as proud, and they set themselves to argue against everything he said. He said at last to them this: "There are many points on which you act contrary to our custom, yea, the custom of the universal Church. Yet, if on three points you will assent to my view, we will tolerate with equanimity all your other practices, though they be contrary to our own. These three points are:—that you celebrate the Passover at its proper time; that you complete the office of baptism, by which we are born again to God, after the manner of the holy Roman and Apostolic Church; that along with us you preach the Word of God to the English race." It is remarkable that he said nothing about their liturgy. Taken in connection with Gregory's free treatment of the question of liturgies, and his alteration of the Roman liturgy itself[1], the fact is very significant.

They then gave their final answer. "They would do none of these things. They would not have him as archbishop[2]: for," they argued among themselves, "if he does not rise to greet us now, he will treat us as of no account at all when we are under his rule." On which Augustine is said to have threatened them by a prophecy that the English would

---

[1] See *The Christian Church in these Islands before the coming of Augustine*, S.P.C.K., 2nd ed., p. 151.

[2] Cadfan was king of part of Wales at this time. He is said to have remarked, when he heard that the Romans had customs which differed from the customs of the British, but they held the same faith, "If the Cymry believe all that Rome believes, that is as strong a reason for Rome obeying us as for us obeying Rome." His grandson Cadwaldr set up his (Cadfan's or Cataman's) epitaph at Llangadwaldr, and there it still remains: *Catamannus rex sapientissimus opinatissimus omnium regum*, "Cataman, the King, the wisest and most thought-of of all kings."

destroy them. So natural a prophecy was in due course fulfilled.

With regard to the demand that they should fulfil, or complete, the office of baptism, *ut ministerium baptizandi compleatis*, according to the custom of the Roman Church, some say that it was the question of three immersions which was raised; others that it was the question of proceeding at once to confirmation, as soon as the child or the convert had been baptized. These are more or less of the nature of guesses. The one thing sure which we have is contained in a letter from Pope Zachary to Boniface of Mentz in 748. He says that from the time of Augustine it was declared in England that baptism without the invocation of the Holy Trinity was not valid; and that the omission of the name of any one of the Three Persons was fatal to the validity of the rite.

And so the hope of a union with the ancient Church of the land came to an end. How often we see, at a great crisis, the power for good, or for evil, that is exercised unconsciously by the personality of a great man. And again, how often we see that some natural defect in a man's character shews itself just when he is close upon success, and destroys his usefulness. And, once again, how often we see that the kindly courtesy of a naturally sympathetic disposition is worth more than a great deal of sound and drastic argument. To any one who has watched the manners of men, as shewn, for instance, at committee meetings and so on, there is something irresistibly natural in the remark, that when the Britons saw how Augustine treated them, they set themselves to argue against all that he said. We see it, sometimes, put down in the case of these British bishops to the ancient British temperament. If that be sound, then a good many persons of my acquaintance possess — or are possessed by — the ancient British temperament. On the other hand, it must be allowed that we still rear a good many Augustines, both in Church and in State.

I have now mentioned, I think, everything which Bede tells us of the doings of Augustine and his companions, except in the matter of church building or restoration in Canterbury, from their arrival in the Isle of Thanet in 596-7 to the last year of Augustine's life, 604-5, which was also the last year of Gregory the Great. Augustine had done what he could to carry out Gregory's metropolitical idea, by his endeavour to obtain recognition from the bishops of the non-English parts of the island.

Not of the whole island, however, by any means; there is no evidence that he knew anything at all of the Christian Church in the northern parts, or in the other island, Ireland[1]. Success with the British bishops would have opened up possibilities, which under a statesman-archbishop might have meant a magnificent creation, nothing less than one great Church of these islands, that in God's Providence were to dominate the greater half of the world; a united Church of England, Scotland, Ireland, and the Isles. Failure with the British bishops stopped the birth of those possibilities, so far as we have seen, or now can see, for ever.

There remained the narrower work of creating a metropolitical see, with diocesan bishops, in the south-east of England, a very small portion of the whole area committed to Augustine's charge. Gregory had specially emphasised the importance of London and York, guided possibly by the facts of past history, still remembered in secular Rome, and not by the actual state of those cities in his time. We are not told that Augustine

---

[1] Unless his invitation to "the bishops or doctors of the *nearest* province of the Britons" implies that he had some inkling of a wider field. It may mean *neighbouring*.

made any enquiry about York. But as regards London he did, in this last year of his life, take a definite step. He established the see, which was, in their intention, to take the place of his own see, as the metropolitical see of the south, when he himself should have passed away.

"The metropolis of the East Saxons," Bede says, speaking of his own time, "is London, an emporium of many nations, that come to it by land and by sea; it is situated on the banks of the Thames, which separates the kingdom of the East Saxons from the kingdom of Kent." In Augustine's time, the East Saxons were reigned over by Sabert, who, in common with all the eastward English up to the Humber, was under the lordship of Ethelbert of Kent. There was this further and closer connection, that Sabert's mother, Ricula, was Ethelbert's sister. To provide for the Christianising of the East Saxons, Augustine proceeded to his first consecration. Alone he consecrated Mellitus, one of the supplementary party sent by Gregory, and therefore not one of those who had played the coward at Aix; he consecrated him to be bishop of the East Saxons. In the course of time, this province received the word of God; and thereupon

King Ethelbert built in London the Church of St. Paul, where Mellitus and his successors should have their episcopal see. There is nothing to suggest that this took place in Augustine's lifetime, and the date usually given to the erection of the church, and the gift of the manor of Tillingham, which we still hold, for the support of the fabric, is 609, four years after Augustine's death. This is the first known dedication in England of any church to either of the Apostles St. Peter and St. Paul alone. The instinct which led to the dedication of the first metropolitical Church of the English, as Gregory meant it to be, to the great Apostle of the Gentile world, was unquestionably sound. The Roman mission took possession of the new land first of all in the name of the Saviour, by their dedication of the episcopal church of Canterbury, and then in the name of St. Paul. If England is dedicated to either of the Apostles St. Peter and St. Paul, after our Lord and only Saviour, it is dedicated to St. Paul. There is, by the way, no real evidence that the west monastery on Thorn-ey, a little higher up the river, was dedicated to St. Peter for long enough after this time.

At the same time—but his name is mentioned after that of Mellitus—Justus, another of the supplementary party, was consecrated by Augustine as bishop in Kent, to reside at the ancient city of Durobrevis, which the English had named Hrofscaster, from a great man among them in very early times, by name Hrof. Here also Ethelbert built a church, probably before St. Paul's, for Kent was already converted before the consecration of Justus. The church was dedicated to St. Andrew, as to which I have more to say soon.

With regard to all of these three episcopal sees, Canterbury, London, and Rochester, Bede says that King Ethelbert made many gifts for the bishops of the sees, and also gave lands and property for the maintenance of those about the bishops. That is, he endowed, as we should say, the bishop, the chapter, and work in the diocese. And, as we are told by those who have studied the general question of the income and property of the Anglo-Saxon kings, he could only deal with his own property. It was, like Peter's pence later, a gift affecting the personal property of the king as head of his family, not what we should call the property of the State. It corresponds to a personal gift by Queen

Victoria, not to a gift by Parliament and Queen combined.

The phrases in Ethelbert's charter to St. Andrew of Rochester seem clearly to point to this personal character of the gifts. He addresses himself in the opening lines of the charter to Eadbald his son, as if recognising that he was giving away a part of what would have come to him, and also, in all probability, recognising him as sub-king, with his royal residence there. In the charter, he says [1], "I give to thee, Saint Andrew, and to thy church in the city Hrofibrevis, a small portion of my land (*aliquantulum telluris mei*)." And again, "This is the boundary of my gift." And, "If any one desires to supplement this donation may the Lord add to him good days." Finally, it was solemnly ratified and made firm—"This, with the counsel of Laurence the bishop and of all my chief men, I have confirmed with the sign of the holy Cross, and I have ordered them to do the like. Amen." That these gifts were to be defended against spoilers, the laws of Ethelbert made clear [2]. The construction of the English language, in its early form, brought about the

---

[1] Haddan and Stubbs, iii. 52.
[2] Ibid., iii. 42.

happy fact, that the first word of the first recorded law passed by an assembly of Englishmen was the word "God."

"These be the dooms that Ethelbert King set in Agustinus days:—

"God's fee and the Church's, xii-fold. Bishop's fee, xi-fold. Priest's fee, ix-fold. Deacon's fee, vi-fold. Clerk's fee, iii-fold."

Those were the restitutions which spoilers of the property of God, of the Church, and of the ministers thereof, must make. This order of gravity of offences is in itself eloquent of right thinking.

And now the time came for Augustine to take his last look at his handiwork. Kent was won to Christ. He had a man at work, endeavouring to win to Christ the neighbouring kingdom. And that was all. No Britons joining forces with them. No twelve bishops under London. No one at York, still less any twelve bishops under him. Drawn so, and it is usually so drawn, the picture is a sad one; and it is on that picture that Augustine took his last look in life. But those who thus estimate the size of his work disregard the dominant fact of its shortness. When was a larger work done in a shorter time than his conversion of Ethelbert and of all the kingdom of Kent, the most powerful kingdom in this land? He had in all about seven years in which to work, from his first landing to his death. Four years certainly went in the conversion of Kent, the ceremonies of his consecration, the consolidation of the work in Kent, the deliberations which led to the drawing up of what I have described as the charter of the Church of the English. About the end of the year 602 he may have begun to act upon it. How long will you allow for all the complicated arrangements, all the difficult negotiations, necessary as preliminaries to those two meetings with the British bishops? And that in an age when the time spent in travel was governed, not by trains averaging forty miles an hour, but by pack-horses averaging less than three; with all the other tardinesses of which this proportion is only a hint? And how long will you give any elderly man to recover from the fatigues of such a journey as none of us, I suppose, has ever made, and to gather up his spirits again for further exertion after such a failure? All this, and the establishment of an additional bishop and bishopric in Kent, and of a missionary bishop in another pagan kingdom, has to be crowded into two years and a fraction of a year. It is vastly easier for any of us to say how little he ever did, than to do more in the time.

As for his character, my remarks will have indicated what I think of that. Of course he had his faults, and they were grave faults. If, being a man, he had not had faults, what sort of kinship with him could you or I have felt?

He was buried in 605, outside the city of Canterbury, close by the abbey church which he had begun to build there; not in or near his own cathedral church, for there were no burials then within a city. This abbey church of St. Peter and St. Paul was finished and consecrated after his death, and then his body was placed in its northern porticus, that is, on the side where St. Augustine's College now stands.

The Abbat Albinus sent to Bede a copy of the epitaph then on the tomb, a hundred years after Augustine's death. When it was placed there, we do not know—

"Here rests the Lord Augustine, first Archbishop of Canterbury, who was sent hither erewhile by the blessed Gregory, pontiff of the Roman city, and being supported by God with the working of miracles, brought Ethelbert the king and his nation from the worship of idols to the faith of Christ, and, the days of his ministry being fulfilled in peace, died on the twenty-sixth day of May, in the reign of the same king."

I propose now to group together the several dedications of churches in England, mentioned in the time of Augustine and his companions, and to endeavour to trace the connection between them and dedications with which the members of the Italian mission may have been familiar in Rome. This will also be an opportunity for speaking of the church-building done or begun in Canterbury by Augustine himself, a subject which I have intentionally left till now.

The first church mentioned is that of St. Martin, at Canterbury. As I understand Bede, this church was not dedicated to St. Martin by the Italian mission, and it certainly was not built, or dedicated to the service of God, by them. It had been used for years before their time by Queen Bertha, as her place of worship, the services being performed by her chaplain-bishop Luidhard and the staff of assistants whom I think he must have had with him; some of whom I dare say were still in Canterbury when Augustine came, though the bishop himself must, it seems, have been dead by that time.

This church, Bede tells us, was "anciently erected to the honour of St. Martin, while the Romans still inhabited Britain." Last year I spoke[1] of the difficulty which has been suggested, namely, that St. Martin only died about 397, while the Roman troops left Britain in 407, and 409 is the date assigned to the end of the Roman empire here. But the phrase "while the Romans were still in the land" may fairly be taken to extend a good deal beyond the technical abandonment of Britain. There is no difficulty at all, to my mind, in supposing that St. Martin's was a Roman temple, or a secular Roman building, in Durovernum, converted to the purposes of a Christian church after 397, or a building then newly erected for a church; in either case dedicated to the famous saint of Tours, by far the most prominent figure[2] among the Christians of Gaul, who were so near of kin to the Britons. This dedication may well have taken place as late as the visit of Germanus, in 429.

---

[1] *The Christian Church in these Islands before the coming of Augustine*, S.P.C.K., 2nd ed., p. 25, note.

[2] For the prevalence of dedications to St. Martin, see p. 113 of the little book last quoted.

But for the clearness of Bede's language, it would have been exceedingly natural to credit Luidhard with this very appropriate dedication. St. Martin's greatest work was the conversion of the Pagans in Gaul. A Gallican bishop, coming to the pagans in England, might well come in the name of Christ and St. Martin.

And again, but for Bede's statement, it would have been very easy to see that no dedication was more likely to have seemed right to the Italians themselves. They were steeped in consciousness of the fact that their forerunner in pagan conversion, in these far parts of the old Roman province of the Galliae, was this very Martin. His miracles filled a very large place in men's minds. They filled four books out of seven of the history of miracles by Gregory of Tours, and Gregory of Tours had only been dead a year or two. The Italians had left, on the Esquiline, the famous church in which Pope Sylvester held a Council in the year 325, when the Church in Rome accepted the decrees of the Council of Nicaea. Upon this church, which still exists as a crypt, Pope Symmachus in 500 had superposed another church, and in that church reposed the relics of Pope Sylvester himself and of St. Martin. I am aware that there is a difference of opinion as to this St. Martin, but I take it to be St. Martin of Tours. Relics of Pope Martin, of whom I do not find a declaration that he was sainted, no doubt were brought to Rome, and placed in this church, probably because it already bore the name of Martin. Who that has enjoyed the privilege of visiting the ancient churches of Rome, does not remember, as standing out prominently among the most venerable things he saw, the Confessio in which those relics still repose, in the church of S. Martino ai Monti?

Some considerable time after the arrival of the Italian mission, probably about the year 602, when Augustine had set up his episcopal seat in Canterbury, he recovered within the city, by the king's help, a church, built, as he had been informed, in old times by Christians of the Roman race. This is a second example of the existence of a pre-Anglian church in or near the royal city of Kent. We are not told that there was any tradition as to its original dedication. Indeed, I am not sure that we are obliged to assume that it had a dedication to any particular saint. It was a Christian church, dedicated to the service of God, and that may have been all, in the very early time to which the record throws us back.

This church Augustine dedicated to the Holy Saviour, our Lord God Jesus Christ. It was his episcopal church, the church of his see.

There can be no doubt as to the reason of this dedication to the Saviour, apart from the obvious fitness of the dedication of their first church to Him in whose name the missionaries taught. In June, 1893, the Romans in England with great ceremony performed "the renewal of the dedication of England to St. Mary and St. Peter." Augustine's dedication was to the Saviour Himself; and "Christ Church," the cathedral church of Canterbury, still remains, the material first-fruits of Augustine's mission, the outward sign of the dedication of England to our Lord Jesus Christ.

Apart from the fitness, there was a definite reason for Augustine's action. He had been Prior of St. Andrew's on the Caelian Hill, at the western extremity of the hill, and from that home many of his party came. At the eastern end of the Caelian, three-quarters of a mile away from St. Andrew's, was the great church of Rome, *omnium urbis et orbis eccle-*

siarum mater et caput, as the inscription at either side of the entrance still tells us, "the mother and head of all the churches of the city and the world." We know it as St. John Lateran, but that is not its ancient name. The old home of the magnificent Laterani, so splendidly improved and decorated in the third century, had passed into the hands of the emperors, and had become an imperial residence. It descended to Fausta, the daughter of the Emperor Maximian, and she brought it to Constantine on her marriage with him in 307. On her death Constantine gave it to Melchiades, the Bishop of Rome, and the grant was confirmed to Silvester, when it became the episcopal residence. Constantine and Silvester built within its vast precincts the great basilica, named from the former owners of the place "the Lateran." It was dedicated to the Saviour, and even as late as 1133, when Innocent II crowned Lothaire and Richildis there, it was still called the Church of the Saviour. Its name of St. John came to it in a curious manner. The deacon Hilary, who was one of the representatives of Leo I at the Robber-Council of Ephesus in 449, the one who so courageously faced the episcopal and secular violence of that infamous assembly, escaped from Ephesus by unfrequented ways, and vowed that if he got safe away he would dedicate a sanctuary to St. John the Evangelist. He did get safe away. Twelve years later he became pope, and he then added a chapel on either side of the Baptistery at the Lateran, the one to St. John the Evangelist, the other to St. John the Baptist. The dedication to the Saviour was probably enlarged by the addition of these saints about the year 900, when the nave was rebuilt after destruction by an earthquake. The most recent writer on the history of this great church[1] is inclined to believe that from Hilary's time the two Saints John were included in the dedication; but there is no evidence that in Augustine's time there was any dedication beyond that to the Saviour. Thus we may take it that Augustine exactly followed at Canterbury the dedication of the "mother and chief church" of the Western world. It is still the chief church of Rome, and its chapter takes precedence of the chapter of St. Peter's. The modern Roman ecclesiastics, however, who in their turn complain bitterly of the Italian Government, are sadly

---

[1] Rohault de Fleury, *Le Latran au Moyen Âge*. Paris, 1877.

modernising Rome. Before 1870 the popes were consecrated at the Lateran, but that crowning ceremony has been removed to St. Peter's. And up to very recent times the apse of Constantine had remained, through all the changes the basilica has seen, even through the rebuilding which modernised all the rest. To Pius IX and Leo XIII we owe the destruction of that last relic of the better times, and the characteristic replacing of the old and pure apse by the present gaudy chancel. We at St. Paul's are new throughout. We are still two years, nearly three, off our two hundredth anniversary. But at least our newness is not of the will of man. St. Paul's in the City of London and San Paolo fuori le mura in Rome have the plea for their newness that they were destroyed by fire. St. Peter's in Rome and the modern chancel of the "mother church of the city and the world" have no such excuse. There are enemies as bad as fire, when an old church is in question.

It was perhaps with direct reference to the association of Constantine's baptistery and a chapel of St. John Baptist with the great basilica of the Saviour in Rome, that Archbishop Cuthbert of Canterbury, between 740 and 758, added at the east of his cathedral church of the Saviour, and almost touching it, a church of St. John Baptist. It was to be used as a baptistery, and as a place in which certain judicial trials, that used to take place in the cathedral church, might be held. It is a singular coincidence, that, at the time when this lecture is delivered, we are considering the propriety of exactly this combination in the chapel which until last year was occupied by the Wellington monument. The removal of the font to the western end of the south-west chapel, the eastward parts continuing to be used as the consistorial court of the bishop of London, would be strictly in accordance with this precedent of early times. In the cathedral church of Canterbury, as Eadmer tells us, it was in the chapel formed by the lowest storey of the south tower that certain cases received judgment, namely, " all disputes from the whole kingdom, which could not be legally referred to the king's court, or to the hundreds or counties."

We come next to the foundation and dedication of the great abbey church of Canterbury, St. Peter and St. Paul, called later, as the ruins still are called, St. Augustine's.

The mention of Archbishop Cuthbert forms a fitting introduction to this part of our story.

When Archbishop Cuthbert was dying, in 758, he devised and carried out—so far as rested with him—a plan for the aggrandisement of the cathedral church at the expense of its great rival, the abbey church of St. Augustine's, or St. Peter and St. Paul as its original dedication was [1]. The monks of St. Augustine's had the right of burying within their precincts the bodies of the archbishops of Canterbury, and the fees and the offerings were of considerable importance. Cuthbert determined that this right should be invaded. Having got the king's permission, he had a stone coffin prepared. When death was near, he summoned the monks, and revealed his plan. They were to conceal his death till they had had time to bury him in the cathedral church itself. Then they were to ring his knell, and great would be their triumph when the insolent people from St. Augustine's came to claim his body for burial. It all fell out accordingly, and to this day we have the expressions of baffled rage in which the rival monks let off their feelings.

Some preface of that kind is necessary to explain a rather remarkable phenomenon.

[1] St. Augustine was added to the dedication in Dunstan's time, 961-988.

Bede once in his History, and only once, mentions the boy martyr of Diocletian's persecution, Pancratius; and that, only in quoting the letter from Pope Vitalian to king Oswin on the death of Wighard in 665, in which the pope says that he is sending relics of seven martyrs, among them Pancratius. But in the records of the monastery of St. Peter and St. Paul, whose foundation and dedication Bede describes, Pancratius played a large part, though Bede does not in the most distant way refer to that fact. Bede got his information about the early history of Christianity in Canterbury from Albinus, the Abbat of St. Peter and St. Paul, or as we now call it, St. Augustine's, and from Nothelm the archpresbyter of London, who was archbishop of Canterbury at Bede's death. In the time of Albinus the rivalry between the two monastic foundations, the cathedral church of the Saviour, and the abbey church of St. Peter and St. Paul, was certainly in full existence. But Albinus was a man of fine character, as was Nothelm also, and I think they were to be trusted to give an unbiassed account. Acting on their report, Bede enters upon no controversial question as between the two establishments. This may have been because he did not know; it had not been explained to him. It may have been because, though he knew, he preferred to pass it by. He merely tells us, first, as to the cathedral church, that Augustine recovered an old church in the city and dedicated it to the Saviour, and there he and all his successors to Bede's time made their habitation. And then, in the next sentence, he tells us that Augustine made also a monastery, not far from the city on the east, in which the king built from the foundations the church of the blessed Apostles St. Peter and St. Paul, where the archbishops of Canterbury and the kings of Kent might be buried; no doubt with a view to the all but universal custom of those times, not to bury within the walls either of a church or of a city. And that is all he tells us of the foundation of the rival institutions, whose mutual strifes lasted for centuries and made some important marks on history. I called attention last year[1] to the fact that the dedication was beyond all question clearly stated as being to St. Peter and St. Paul, whereas Cardinal Vaughan and all the Roman Catholic bishops living in England solemnly

[1] See *The Church in these Islands before the coming of Augustine*, p. 16.

declared, on the occasion of "the renewal of the dedication of England to St. Mary and St. Peter," that the second monastery of Canterbury "was dedicated to St. Peter himself." This statement, made for a highly controversial purpose, is more and worse than a *suppressio veri*. Truly history repeats itself, in the Roman Church as elsewhere, and not always the most creditable history.

The historians of St. Augustine's have a fuller account. Taking Thorn as fairly representing their traditions, we learn that the king gave to Augustine his palace in the city, which he "recovered into a church," restored to the purposes of a church, and dedicated to the Saviour. Between Christ Church within the city and St. Martin's some distance outside, on the road to Richborough, there was, still without the city, a pagan shrine, where the king used to worship his idol. This place the king gave to Augustine, who broke the idol, cleansed the building, "converted it from a synagogue to a church," and dedicated it to Saint Pancratius. "And this," he adds, "was the first church dedicated by Augustine," thus giving it precedence over Christ Church in point of date. There was still in his time the altar at which Augustine celebrated the

Mass, on the spot where the altar of the demon had stood, and there were the marks on the wall outside where the demon in his impotent wrath scratched furrows in the stone with his talons. This altar was in a chapel on the south side of the church. Gregory, we may here note, had written to Ethelbert that he must overthrow the heathen temples; but on second thoughts, or on fuller information, he wrote to the mission that where the temples were well built and useful, they should be cleansed, and dedicated as churches. It was in this letter, to Mellitus, that he laid down the policy which has resulted in our having so many customs which are descendants of pagan solemnities. "They have been accustomed to offer in sacrifice many oxen to demons. Give them some Christian commemoration to take the place of this; say, on the dedication day of the church, formerly a temple, or on the festival of the martyr whose relics are there. Let them build their booths of boughs, and kill their cattle, and eat them; but make it a Christian feast, a thanksgiving to the Lord of all."

Pancratius was a boy of fourteen, who offered himself for a martyr's death in Rome, during the persecution by Diocletian, and was martyred at a place on the west of the city, outside all the walls, where the church dedicated in his name stands. It was dedicated by Pope Symmachus about the year 505, and there is a direct connection of Pope Gregory with it, in the fact that he gave it to the Benedictines. It is of course far away from his own part of the city, not in the city at all, and across the river; some two miles away from the monastery of St. Andrew's, and nearly three from the Lateran. But the record was, that Gregory's own house, out of which he founded the monastery of St. Andrew's, stood on ground which had been the property of Pancratius, and this would naturally give to all of them, from Gregory downwards, a special interest in the youthful martyr. It has been suggested, too, that in the mind of Augustine there might be some connection of idea between the boy Pancratius and the Yorkshire boys who had turned Gregory's attention to the English, but that is, I think, too far-fetched as a reason for the dedication.

But we have not finished with Thorn and the site of the pagan fane. On this property, he tells us, the king built a church in honour of St. Peter and St. Paul. Thus here the two accounts are at one again. Bede tells us it was built from the foundations, clearly intending to say that it was not an old building restored, as others were; and here he may have a veiled reference to the adjacent St. Pancras. It is certain that to this day there are very interesting and considerable remains of the ancient Roman building converted into the church of St. Pancras. They stand to the east of the great ruins of the abbey, and to the south of the axis line of that church. The south side, on which, we are told, was the porticus with the altar where Augustine offered the Mass on the very spot where Ethelbert's idol had stood, is the part most clearly seen. There, half-way between east and west, is still the square porticus, or chapel, of Roman brick, and in it is still the altar, placed centrally on the east side. The scratches of the demon's talons have disappeared; they are said to be shewn to unwary visitors at a different part of the building, in a less ancient wall.

Some years ago, under a stone at the west entrance to this very ancient church, a leaden casket was found, containing a small number of human bones. It had an inscription on it of very ancient date, reported to be not legible.

The bones were reverently buried again in their own place, and from this their long resting-place they were soon after most irreverently stolen. There are some uncomfortable modern stories, current among those who know, of this stealing of relics. In the early middle ages it was regarded as a virtuous act.

The dedication to St. Peter and St. Paul was obviously the one to come next after that to the Saviour. The earliest Saints' Day of the Christian Church was that of St. Peter and St. Paul. St. Paul's intimate connection with Rome has the certainty of scriptural authority. A metaphor of much disputed meaning is the only trace of St. Peter's connection with Rome in the New Testament; but I suppose that all the Christian world is willing to accept the later story of his martyrdom in Rome, which does not require any considerable residence there. Many, as we know, believe that he lived long in Rome, in accordance with a legend coming from a source tainted with heresy. And many maintain that he was actually bishop of Rome, playing havoc with the earliest and best records. Some explain St. Paul's remarkable silence about St. Peter's connection with Rome, and the silence of the Acts of the Apostles, which certainly clamour for explanation, by the supposition that he happened to be absent from Rome at the times of which St. Paul and St. Luke wrote. The modern Roman of London has told us gravely that he was living in Britain at the time; and he is placed at the head of the Roman "chart," as the founder of the Christian Church in this island. But leaving all that, early Rome naturally coupled together the two names of Peter and of Paul, described them as the *principes*, the chief or princes of the Apostles, called them the founders of the Church of Rome. We need look no further for a reason of this dedication. Peter, who accompanied Laurentius on the mission from Augustine to Rome, was the first abbat of St. Peter and St. Paul. He was sent, later, on a mission to Gaul, and was drowned at Amfleat (Ambleteuse, near Boulogne) in 607. Rufinianus, who was one of the supplementary party, eventually succeeded to the abbacy, and died in 626.

At the time of Ethelbert's death, a chapel or *porticus* of St. Martin had been added to the church, and in it both Bertha and Ethelbert were buried. In the cathedral church, too, there was a chapel of St. Martin, at the base of the tower on the north side of the nave. It is interesting to notice this repeated recognition of the soldier saint, Martin, in the earliest days of a nation which was eventually to adopt St. George as its patron saint.

It may be as well to finish with the Canterbury dedications, though that course will have the effect of placing out of chronological order the dedications at Rochester and London, which in point of time came next to those already mentioned.

Ethelbert's son built in this same monastery of St. Peter and St. Paul yet another church, in honour of "the holy mother of God," which Archbishop Mellitus consecrated. It was built as a sign of his penitence, when he returned to, or accepted, the faith. Thorn tells us that when the great church was enlarged, this church of St. Mary, which lay between the first church and the second, that is, St. Pancras and St. Peter and St. Paul, was incorporated in the abbey church as the church in the crypts. Here again there is no difficulty about the dedication. The great basilica of Santa Maria Maggiore, so called because it is the chief of all the churches dedicated to St. Mary in Rome, was already in existence. It was founded in 352 by Liberius, the pope whose acceptance of a semi-Arian creed is so serious a difficulty in the maintenance of the most recent addition to the many added dogmas of modern Rome. To its founder it owed the name of Basilica Liberiana. It is said to have been the basilica which plays a considerable part in that terrible story of massacre and sacrilege which gathers round the contest of Damasus and Ursicinus, in 366, for the coveted position of Vicar on earth of the Prince of Peace. It is perhaps worth while to give the view which the contemporary historian Ammianus Marcellinus took of this disgraceful contest, when over a hundred corpses of murdered men were dragged from the floor of the basilica. "No wonder that for so magnificent a prize as the bishopric of Rome, men should contest with the utmost eagerness and obstinacy. To be enriched by the lavish donations of the principal females of the city; to ride, splendidly attired, in a stately chariot; to sit at a profuse, luxuriant, more than imperial table; these are the rewards of successful ambition."

The basilica of Santa Maria Maggiore was built to cover the portion of ground on which a miraculous shower of snow fell on the fifth of August, and thence had its early name of Sancta Maria ad Nives. A hundred and sixty or seventy years before Augustine's time it was enlarged by Sixtus III to the dimensions now so well known, a great basilica all nave.

The cathedral church, too, of Saxon times, specially honoured the Blessed Virgin. The Lady Chapel occupied the western apse of the church, the archbishop's chair being at the extreme west, facing east, and the altar being placed on the diameter of the apse; so that, as Eadmer points out, the priest in celebrating faced eastwards, and looked down upon the people in the nave, the oratory of the Virgin being raised some height above the level of the nave, and approached by steps.

While I have mentioned Santa Maria Maggiore as the natural prototype of the church built by Ethelbert's son, we must not forget that on the Caelian itself, very near to St. Andrew's, was another ancient church of St. Mary, Santa Maria della Navicella, or Domnica. This church stood on the house of St. Cyriaca, Dominica or Domnica being the Latin translation of her Greek name. It was itself of sufficient importance to be prominent in the minds of the monks from St. Andrew's, as the house was the traditional place where the deacon Laurentius distributed the treasures of the church among the poor, by order of Pope Xystus II, in the year (257), in which they were both of them martyred under Valerian.

There remains one other church, to be mentioned among those dating from the time of Augustine and his companions. When our refugee ex-bishop of London, Mellitus, was archbishop of Canterbury, a fire broke out. The archbishop was a martyr to the gout, and had to be carried in a chair to the scene of the fire. His presence and his prayers arrested the conflagration, just when it had reached the martyr-church, the memorial of the Four Crowned Martyrs. This is a point of special interest. The Church of the Four Crowned Saints, Quattro Santi Incoronati, is one of the most instructive in Rome, from an archaeological point of view. It was rebuilt in 1111 by Paschal II (who put on record four years later his invaluable complaint of the perfect independence of the Church of England), to replace the church built in honour of the Saints Carpoferus, Severus, Severianus, and Victorinus, by Pope Honorius in 626. This is two or three years later than the mention of the Four Crowned Martyrs at Canterbury; a striking evidence of the community of sentiment between Canterbury and Rome, possibly an indication that Canterbury in this respect set the fashion to Rome. The well-known church in Rome stands within a short half-mile of Gregory's St. Andrew's, across the hill; and thus we have here another hint of the probability that the Italian Mission connected their dedications with those of their own quarter of Rome. From this point of view, however, and indeed from almost any point of view, we cannot help feeling some surprise that we have—so far as we know—nothing in the earliest English Church to connect us with churches so near to St. Andrew's in Rome, and in themselves and in their dedication so important, as S. Stefano Rotondo and S. Clemente.

There still remain to be mentioned the dedications of three cathedral churches in our period, two by Augustine, and one, a generation later, by Paulinus. The two are, St. Andrew's, Rochester, and St. Paul's, London. The third and latest, St. Peter's, York, may wait till we come to the north.

The choice of St. Andrew was very natural. I need make no apology for dwelling upon it, for here we have our finger upon the cradle of the mission that founded the English Church.

The monastery and church of St. Andrew in Rome was founded about 575 by Gregory himself, upon his own property, which, as we have seen, was understood to have been the property of the family of Pancratius, said to be Phrygians. It was on the western slope of the Caelian Hill, facing the Palatine, above the road which led from the Appian Way to the Colosseum, by which our own Paul passed through Rome to the Praetorian Camp. Here was the family mansion of Gregory's ancestors, men of senatorial position and of wealth and importance; including Pope Felix (II or III) his great-grandfather, and the presbyter Felix, the pope's father.

The dedication of the church of St. Andrew at Rome was altered some time after Gregory's death to "St. Gregory." The ancient church itself has disappeared, and the present church was built on the site as late as 1734. But I found in the steps up to the altar in the north aisle a piece of sculpture, which had evidently formed part of one of the sculptured screens of the enclosed choir of the basilica; a remarkably fine example of the imitation of bronze screens in marble, and of a rare design. And in the garden on the north side, I found, used as the riser of a step, one of the grooved and sculptured marble posts which held the slabs of the choir screens. These, we cannot well doubt, are relics of Gregory's own church as built by himself, evidences of the style in which he built, decorative structure on which his eye, perhaps his hand, has rested. The magnificent white marble throne which is shewn in St. Gregory's Church as the chair of Pope Gregory himself is one of the beautiful thrones of Greek sculpture which were brought to Rome in the time of the Empire, and served as seats for the Vestals and other chief personages in the Colosseum and elsewhere. They have found their way to various parts of Rome, but nowhere is there one so fine, I think, as this. Its beauty of sculptured relief is not seen at all, unless, by the great favour which was accorded to me, you get it moved from its position so as to see the back. The rubbing which they allowed me to take of it shews a very fine piece of symmetrical decoration of the best type, when laid out flat. It was in this original church of St. Andrew that Wilfrid saw on the high altar the beautifully ornamented text of the Gospels, which suggested to him the great gift he eventually prepared for his church at Ripon, a book of the Gospels written in letters of gold on sheets of purple vellum, with covers of solid gold set with jewels[1].

That does not exhaust the personal memorials of Gregory which still exist there. In the garden are three chapels, originally built by Gregory, and restored by Cardinal Baronius. One is dedicated to St. Silvia, the mother of Gregory; another to St. Andrew; and the other to St. Barbara. In this last is a great marble table, 11 feet long and 3 feet broad, set on classical Greek supports much resembling in style Pope Gregory's chair. The inscription[2] tells us that this was the dining table at which Gregory was receiving, according to his wont, twelve poor men, when he found one guest more than he had expected—our Lord, in the form of an angel. It was from this legend that the popes used to wait on thirteen pilgrims, instead of twelve on Maundy Thursday. Whatever we may think of the story, there is no doubt that the table and its supports were in existence long before Gregory's time, and may well have been, like the chair, Gregory's own property.

---

[1] See *Lessons from Early English Church History*, S.P.C.K., pp. 59, 112.
[2]   Bis senos Gregorius hic pascebat egentes,
      Angelus et decimus tertius occubuit.

It is impossible for an Englishman to visit this site, even though the buildings are modern and far from magnificent, without feeling that here indeed is the sacred spot on which the foundations of the English Church were conceived and prepared; where the first plans were discussed and matured; where Augustine and several of his companions were trained for their work; and where Gregory no doubt came often, from his neighbouring palace at the other end of the hill, to pray for the men whom he had sent, and the men and the women whom they had won. It was by a very true instinct that when Dr. Manning was made a cardinal, he was made titular of this church, as Cardinal Vaughan now is.

It may be well to add that there came to England, later, a second wave of interest in St. Andrew, which has made a lasting mark. Wilfrid was first introduced to the Christian Art of Rome in St. Andrew's Church. He came home with this first impression printed deep on his mind. To St. Andrew he dedicated the great church which he built on Tyneside, at Hagulstad, the present Hexham, in the year 674, the church of whose construction we have so full an account from his chaplain. Wilfrid's successor Acca was bishop of Hexham from 709 to 732, when he mysteriously disappeared, the belief being that he had gone to establish a bishopric among the Picts. He had acquired relics of St. Andrew. After a few years he returned to Hexham, where he was buried about 740, two great and very nobly sculptured crosses being set up at the head and foot of his grave, one of which we still possess, while the place where the other is buried is known to one or two people. There was in Fife a promontory known to the early Picts as Muic-ross, the promontory of the swine. This name had been changed to Kilrimont, the cell of the king's mount, from a monastery founded there about the year 600. In the time of the Pictish king Hungus, who reigned from 731 to 760, strangers brought to Kilrimont relics of St. Andrew, and the name was then again changed to St. Andrew's. The coincidence of date and of event can scarcely be accidental, and the opinion is gradually making its way, originating in a lucky guess by Dr. Skene, that the cultus of St. Andrew may have come from Hexham to Kilrimont. Thus to Gregory's Church of St. Andrew in Rome, we may possibly trace the patron Saint of Scotland and the Scottish emblem of the St. Andrew's Cross in the Union Jack.

But in the intention of Gregory and Augustine, if indeed Gregory intervened at all in these more domestic affairs of the mission, by far the most important question was, to whom should London be dedicated? London was to be the metropolitan see of the south, with twelve suffragans. When the mission entered upon London, they had indeed come to the central point of their enterprise. In the name of what saint of God should they take possession of this, the foundation-stone, or chief corner-stone, of the Christian edifice among the Gentiles? Certainly in the name of the Apostle of the Gentiles; certainly in the name of St. Paul. Here, if anywhere, was the choice of the patron saint of England. Of the distant shadowy north, with its potential metropolitan and its possible suffragans, they saw no chance of knowing anything more for at least some time to come. When the proper time should come, they might plant there the name of the other of the chief of the Apostles, St. Peter; but here in actual London they planted the name of St. Paul. The great basilica of St. Paul without the walls of Rome was very well known to the monks of St. Andrew's. Many a time they had paced from the Clivus Scauri, the Via S. Gregorio of to-day, by the Baths of Antonine to the Ostian Gate, three-quarters of a mile from their home, and thence to the scene of the martyrdom, where the old men among them remembered to have seen from the walls Totila encamped. Pope Anacletus, that second bishop of Rome who has to be made somehow into a third bishop in order to make room for St. Peter as the first, a process which the stubbornness of historical facts renders very risky, had founded the basilica in the first century, over the catacomb of the Roman lady who buried on her estate the remains of St. Paul. Constantine had enlarged it. In 388 the noble church which was burned down seventy years ago[1] was begun on the same site; in 395 it was completed by Honorius as Augustine knew it; two hundred years after Augustine it was enlarged by Pope Leo. Of this basilica the kings of England were fitly styled the Protectors until the Reformation, as the rulers of Austria were Protectors of the Vatican basilica, France of the Lateran, and Spain of S. Maria Maggiore. It was with the great St. Paul's of Rome in their mind that they came to the

[1] July 16, 1823.

great broad top of the hill of London, and here, high above the water-way of the nations, dedicated to St. Paul, the Apostle of the Gentiles, the Cathedral Church of London; destined to become, as old St. Paul's was till new St. Peter's was built in Rome, the largest church in the Christian world. The incidence of the emphasis which they laid on this dedication has through all changes persisted. Others are "Canterbury," "Rochester," "York"; we are "St. Paul's."

Is it by mere chance that close round this English St. Paul's of ours there clustered the earliest dedications in Kent, and the names of the author and the leader of the mission [1]—St. Martin's, Christ Church, St. Andrew's, St. Gregory's, St. Augustine's?—St. Gregory being the nearest of all.

[1] This was suggested to me by Dr. Fish, Rector of St. Margaret Pattens.

LECTURE IV.

The Canterbury succession. — Laurentius and the Scots. — Mellitus sent by Laurentius to Rome. — Death of Ethelbert. — Paganism of Eadbald and of Sabert's sons. — Flight of Italian bishops to Gaul. — Their return. — Death of Laurentius. — Succession and death of Mellitus. — Succession of Justus. — The pallium again sent. — The conversion of Northumbria. — Consecration of Honorius by Paulinus. — Conversion of the East Angles. — Death of Edwin and flight of Paulinus. — Net result of the Italian Mission. — Act for restraining Appeals to Rome.

BEFORE Augustine died, he took a step which I suppose canonists would call uncanonical. Gregory had taught him not to be too strict. He had realised that the Christian Church, even in Kent, was in a very elementary state, only kept going, only kept together, by his own oversight. It had grown too quickly to be very strong. He feared that if, even for an hour, there should be no spiritual head over the whole, disintegration would set in. How true his estimate was, the strange stories we shall have to tell a little later will shew.

He therefore consecrated Laurentius bishop, to succeed him without an interval. Bede, who had not our opportunities for investigation, and received as gospel what he got from Rome, explains that in this Augustine acted as did "the first pastor of the Church, the most blessed prince of the Apostles, Peter, who, having founded the Church of Christ at Rome, is said to have consecrated Clement as his coadjutor and successor." Fortunately for Bede, he did not know, as we have to know, the endless difficulties into which such a statement plunges the controversialist, difficulties in the aggregate insoluble.

We have seen what Gregory's arrangement had been. Augustine was to be the last person who should govern the Christian Church of England from Canterbury. The bishop of London was to be his successor in metropolitan rank; and for the future, the metropolitan bishop of London was to be consecrated by his own synod. This arrangement had been so recently made, not more than two years ago, or three, that we are compelled to understand Augustine's opinion to have been that the time was not yet come for it to be put in execution. The East Saxons had only made a beginning of conversion. Canterbury must continue to govern till London was ready.

And this only throws up into more prominence the fact that there is no hint of consulting Rome. If Mellitus had succeeded Augustine, it might have been said, and it certainly would have been said, that the order of Gregory was being obeyed. As it was, the spiritual head of the Church of the English acted on his own responsibility, and set up another metropolitan to succeed him, with no more ceremony than the consecration of a bishop. That, if it is a fact, is a very great fact for us, in view of later interferences with our liberty.

Laurentius was one of the original companions of Augustine, one of those who had played the coward at Aix. He was Augustine's most trusted friend, the man chosen to go to Pope Gregory and tell of the consecration of the first bishop of the English, and of the problems that were puzzling him. He presided over the affairs of the Church of the English for fourteen or fifteen years, to the beginning of the year 619.

Laurentius felt, as Bede tells us, that the foundations of the English Church had been nobly laid, and he made it his business to lay them even wider still, and to advance the superstructure. The tradition had come down to Bede that he laboured to build up the work by two main methods, frequent preaching, and the continual example of pious work. But, still following Bede, he not only took care of the new church gathered from among the English—a phrase in itself sufficient to warn us that the real amount of serious conversion was not great—but he endeavoured to bring his pastoral zeal to bear upon the old inhabitants of Britain, and upon the Scots who inhabited Ireland, the island nearest to Britain. It is clear that the importance of existing facts was revealing itself to the Italian mission, and union with the native Christians of the old race was felt to be as valuable, with a broad view for the future, as the attempt to convert directly the native pagans of the new.

Laurentius found that the case of the Scoti in Ireland was much the same as that of the Britons in Britain itself. In many respects their life and profession were not in accordance with ecclesiastical custom. Especially, they, like the Britons, kept the day of the Lord's Resurrection from the 14th to the 20th of the moon. Of course if the 14th day of the moon, that is, the day of full moon, was a Sunday, they were keeping the day of the Resurrection on the day of the Last Supper or on the day of the Crucifixion, according to the usual views of the incidence of those days. He determined, therefore, to write a letter to them, jointly with the other bishops of the English Church, to beseech them to enter into unity with the universal Church.

Unfortunately Bede only gives us the beginning of his letter. The whole letter would, I feel sure, have been exceedingly valuable. This is the letter, as far as we have it:—

"To the lords our very dear brethren the bishops or abbats throughout the land of the Scoti, Laurentius, Mellitus, Justus, bishops, servants of the servants of God.

"When the apostolic see sent us, as its wont has been in all parts of the world, to preach in these western parts to the pagan races, it happened that we entered the country before we were properly acquainted with it. We have venerated both the Britons and the Scoti with great reverence for their sanctity, believing that they walked in the way of the universal Church. But since we have got to know the Britons, we have supposed that the

Scoti were superior to them. Now, however, we have learned by means of Bishop Dagan, who has come to Britain, and of Abbat Columbanus among the Gauls, that they do not differ from the Britons in their manner of life. For when Bishop Dagan came to us, he not only would not take food with us, but would not even take food in the same guesthouse in which we were eating."

That is all that Bede gives us. The address of the letter, "to the bishops or abbats," probably indicates the difficulty which the Italians felt in understanding the Scotic practice. The monasteries were ruled by abbats, and contained bishops, superior to the abbat in point of orders, subject to them as members of the monastery[1]. Of Dagan, who is well known to students of Irish history as a leader of the native school against the Roman school in the matter of Easter, I mentioned last year a very pleasant fact[2]. We have seen how he entirely refused to communicate even in secular food with Laurentius and his party. But in the Stowe Missal we find a very ancient list of persons commemorated, the list which lay on the altar of the church; and there Dagan's

---

[1] *The Church in these Islands before Augustine*, pp. 124, 5.
[2] *Ibid.*, p. 129.

name [1] reposes in peace, next but one to the names of these very men, Laurentius, Mellitus, Justus. It is a Scotic list, not an English one. The Scotic temperament could forgive; whether the English lists forgave or not we do not know. There were, however, things that even the angelic temperament of the Irish Scots did not forgive. They did not enrol the name of Augustine on their altar list.

So far as Bede goes, nothing came of this letter. Gocelin tells us that an Irish archbishop, by name Terenanus, was attracted to England by the fame of Laurentius, and by him converted to the true computation of Easter. I would rather have had the fact from an Irish source; and the phrase "an Irish archbishop," 1300 hundred years ago, tends to disbelief. Terenanus has been identified with a bishop of Armagh.

This was not the only attempt made by Laurentius and his fellow-bishops. They wrote also to the sacerdotes, the priests or bishops, for as I have remarked before [2] the force of the word is disputed, the sacerdotes

---

[1] He was bishop of Inbher-Daoile, if that information means anything to the reader. Put into English spelling, it is Innereilly.

[2] See page 86.

of the Britons, endeavouring to confirm them in catholic unity. But Bede has by this time given up the Britons. He does not give us a word of the letter, or of the response, if any. He merely remarks, "how much good he did by it, the present times still shew." That sentence he left standing when he finished his history. We know that while the Picts of Scotland and the Scots of Ireland had come in to the Roman Easter before 731, where Bede closed his history, the Welsh still stood out. On these matters I said enough last year [1].

I should like to suggest, in passing, for anything that links our present with this distant past has an interest at least, if not a value, that Bede's frequent use of *sacerdos*, in connexion with the Britons, reflects a local colour. The great memorial stone at Kirkmadrine[2] in Galloway, the principal ecclesiastical memorial[3] of British times long before

---

[1] *The Church in these Islands before Augustine*, pp. 152, 3.
[2] *Ibid.*, p. 110.
[3] At Whithorn, where the work of excavating the Priory is under the careful charge of Mr. W. Galloway, to whom archaeologists owe so much, they have found a stone with an inscription of extreme interest, at least as early as that mentioned in the text. It is as follows: *Te Dominum laudamus. Latinus xxxv annorum et filia sua ann. v*

Augustine, uses the same word, *sancti et prae-cipui sacerdotes*. And the regular North British patronymic for the descendant of a priest is Mac Taggart, from Sagert, Tsagert, Taggart.

Having tried to do so much, and done so little, Laurentius determined to refer to Rome on the needs of the Church of the English. We might have supposed that the last person he could afford to send, the last person who could find or make time to go, next to himself, would be the missionary bishop who was supposed to be hard at work among the East Saxons. However that might be, Mellitus went to Rome. Even in these days of ours, with a mail service almost as well managed and as universal as the posting arrangements on the roads of imperial Rome, colonial and missionary bishops find it a saving of time to come to England, and make their way in person to the Board Rooms of the Societies for Missions and for the Promotion of Christian Knowledge. Perhaps Laurentius felt

---

ic sinum fecerunt nepus Barrovadi. "We praise Thee. the Lord. Latinus, 35 years of age, and his daughter, of 5 years, here made their resting-place. Grandson of Barrovad." That, at least, is my rendering. Others do violence to the text, as I think. See also p. 86.

that Rome would attend to Mellitus, but might not answer a letter.

Times were indeed changed since the year when Augustine sent Laurentius to Rome to confer with Pope Gregory. Two new popes had come and gone, Sabinianus and Boniface. Neither is important enough to appear in the index of Robertson's *Church History*. It is rather a pity that they appear anywhere. Happy, they say, is the nation that has no annals. Happier might Rome be if there were no annals for the 101 years that followed the death of Gregory the Great. Twenty-eight popes in 101 years, a little more than three years and a half each, does not promise well for useful work; and the period embraces the heresy of Honorius and the martyrdom—for it was nothing less—of Martin.

Mellitus found Gregory's memory and Gregory's works at a discount in Rome. Scandalous scenes had been enacted on Gregory's death. His profuse gifts to the poor were declared by his successor Sabinianus, a hard and avaricious man, to have been prodigal waste of the treasures of the Church, for the purchase of personal popularity. And, again, he was charged with having defaced and destroyed many of the glories of art in Rome by overthrowing temples and breaking up statues. The people rose in wrath to destroy what there was left of Gregory, his writings, his library. But Peter the Deacon—that is, the archdeacon—in zeal for Gregory, asserted in the pulpit that he had himself seen the Holy Ghost in the form of a dove whispering in Gregory's ear as he wrote. Peter died in the pulpit as he was confirming this with an oath, and the people took that as a sign from heaven that what he had said was true; and so the library was spared. The spirit of Gregory three times came back to earth and remonstrated with Sabinianus, and on a fourth occasion struck him so violent a blow on the head that he died; and his funeral procession had to get round to St. Peter's outside the walls, so great was the tumult in Rome.

Boniface, who succeeded him, is famed in story as the pope who assumed that title of universal bishop, of which our great Gregory had declared that its assumption betokened the coming of antichrist[1]. He was a small man for so great a title. Another Boniface came next, and he it was who received Mellitus. Bede notes that it was this Boniface who obtained from the Emperor Phocas per-

---

[1] See page 15.

mission to convert the Pantheon into a Christian church. Lest this mention of the Eastern Emperor should surprise us, at this relatively late date, it is well to bear in mind that a pope of Rome was not rightly pope till his appointment was confirmed by the Emperor, and that, as we know, went on for centuries, under Easterns and under Germans. The idea of a secular ruler being in this most important sense supreme, was not left for Henry VIII to invent.

Mellitus found a synod of Italian bishops collected in Rome, and he sat among them. In later times, England was thought of such supreme importance to the Roman see, that the archbishop of Canterbury sat on the pope's right hand at a Council, and the archbishop of York on his left. The acts of this synod, and the letters of Boniface to Laurentius and to Ethelbert, all of which Mellitus is said to have brought to England, are only represented by vague and unauthoritative statements. The object of the synod was to treat of the position of monks; and Mellitus was invited to attend that he might by his subscription give the confirmation of his authority to whatever might be regularly decreed.

We now come to one of the most dramatic events in the history of the Italian mission.

Ethelbert died, Bede tells us, in 616; the day is understood to have been February 24. But he adds that this was twenty-one years after his conversion, which would make the year 618. He was buried in the porticus, or transeptal chapel, of St. Martin, within the Church of the blessed Apostles St. Peter and St. Paul, where also Queen Bertha was buried. Bede mentions as one special point among benefits conferred by him, that he made decrees after the Roman fashion, written in English, which were still observed in Bede's time, first among them being the law of restitution for theft of Church property, which I have already given [1].

The death of Ethelbert brought on a great crisis. His son Eadbald had been unwilling— meaning, clearly, had refused—to accept the faith of Christ. On his father's death he carried out the pagan custom of his race, and took to wife the young widow left by his father, who had married again on Bertha's death; her name is given in some lists as Emma. Gregory had expressly forbidden this, in his answers to Augustine, as a heinous crime.

[1] See page 115.

He had also forbidden marriage with a brother's widow, on the like ground of "one flesh," but a later pope allowed Henry VIII to contract that so-called marriage, and another pope was found to declare it valid. I do not find that Augustine thought it necessary to ask, or Gregory to volunteer, an opinion as to the marriage of an uncle with a full niece, an incestuous union which produced so profound a revulsion, even in Constantinople of all places, in the case of the Emperor Heraclius and his niece Martina, in these times of which we have to speak. It has been allowed in our own time by Pope Leo XIII.

This open declaration of full paganism of course encouraged those who only from fear or favour had professed Christianity in Ethelbert's time; and the restrictions imposed by the purer faith were openly violated. There was a reaction in favour of the old licence. The young king—we do not know what his age was, I believe—was subject, Bede tells us, to attacks of madness.

About the same time Sabert also died, the king of the East Saxons, leaving three sons, Sered, Seward, and Sigebert. The worship of idols had for a short time before Sabert's death been discontinued, a sign that Mellitus had only after long effort, in twelve years, gained so much of his point. The sons of Sabert reverted to idol worship, and gave their people free licence to do the same, and they did not long leave Mellitus in peace. They came to him when he was celebrating the solemnities of the Mass and giving the Eucharist to the people. According to the common report, they said to him, puffed up by the pride of barbarians, "Why do you not give to us, too, that fine bread, which you used to give to our father Saba" (for that had been their name for him) "and have not now ceased to give to the people in the Church?" To this he replied, "If you will be washed clean in that saving font in which your father was washed clean, you can partake of that holy bread of which your father partook. But if you contemn the laver of life, you can certainly not receive the bread of life." They said, "We will not to enter that font, for we have no knowledge that we need it; all the same, we will to be refreshed with that bread."

This demand was repeated over and over again, and Mellitus, of course, never gave any sign of yielding. The young men at last lost all patience, and declared that if he would not oblige them in so small and easy a matter, he should not remain in their province; and they drove him out.

He went naturally, in his despair, to Canterbury. Justus was summoned from Rochester, and the three bishops anxiously discussed the situation. To whom shall we liken them? Cranmer, shall we say, Latimer, and Ridley, when the question was of burning? It was "decreed by common consent," exactly the phrase employed to describe the coward-conference at Aix, to abandon their purpose and go home, exactly the conclusion of that conference. Then, it was the argument of *tutius*, "safer," to give it up; now, it was *satius*, "better worth while," to go home. But from our point of view, as representing the English side of the question, the interest centres upon the main fact, on which they were agreed, that their work up to that time was practically fruitless. "It was better worth while for the whole party to go home, and there serve God with free mind, than to live, to no purpose, among barbarians who rebelled against the faith." "Tutius" is the motto of the Romans under discouragement at Aix, "satius" of the Romans under discouragement at Canterbury. Neither is a missionary's word. Mellitus and Justus at once made off to Gaul, and there awaited the end.

Laurentius made all his preparations for joining them. On the last night he had his bed laid in the Church of St. Peter and St. Paul, having, it would seem, got away from his official residence in the city, and gone to the abbey to be clear of the gates and to be on the road to Richborough. About thirty-five years later, Pope Martin, under circumstances of extreme danger, had his bed laid before the altar in the Lateran, not deserting, as Laurentius had done, the Church of the Saviour. But the end was very different in the two cases. To Laurentius, in his bed, the prince of the apostles appeared. Long time in the secret of the night he flogged him with most stringent scourges, and kept asking him, with apostolic sharpness, " Would he forsake the flock? Who was to take charge of them? Had he forgotten his example,—chains, scourgings, prisons, afflictions, death, the death of the cross, to be crowned with Christ?" We seem to hear in the short sharp questions, in the balance of the words, the rhythmic swish of the descending lash.

The scourging and the exhortation put

courage into Laurentius,—as Bede says, animated him. As soon as it was day he went to the king, and opening his robe shewed the lacerated flesh. The king asked in astonishment, who had dared so to treat a man of such position? When the matter was explained to him, he was greatly afraid; he forswore his idols, dismissed his wife, became a Christian, was baptized, and became an active supporter of the Church. The personal part played by St. Peter here and at the synod of Whitby is an interesting and indeed the principal feature in both stories.

Eadbald sent over to France, recalled Mellitus and Justus, and bade them return to their churches. This Justus did, after an absence estimated at about a year. But London preferred the idolatrous pontiffs, and would not admit Mellitus, who lived, we suppose, at Canterbury. Eadbald was not the great man his father Ethelbert had been, and the East Saxons would not listen to him.

Not long after this, Laurentius died, February 2, 619. He was succeeded naturally by Mellitus, the bishop or ex-bishop of the East Saxons, nothing being said of any formalities. Again an independent action of the English Church. Justus continued to work at Rochester. London was left to its idols. The extinction of the fire in Canterbury by his presence, already described, is the one special fact of the archiepiscopate of Mellitus recorded by Bede. He died on April 24, 624.

Justus, bishop of Rochester, at once succeeded to the archiepiscopate, again without mention of any formalities. This is the third case of a succession to Canterbury without any mention of Rome. The charter of our national independence was being written deep on living history.

At this very moment it was that Rome made a forward step. Boniface IV, the host of Mellitus, had come and gone. The Roman Deusdedit, forerunner in name of our own Deusdedit, the first Englishman to become archbishop of Canterbury (655-668), Pope Deusdedit had come and gone. Yet another Boniface, the fifth, had come; and he in turn was on the point of going, to make way for the catastrophe of Pope Honorius; that fundamental shaking, whose tremblings are still severely felt, and always will be, when the Roman claims are forced upon the attention of the students of history. Just in the lull before this great storm, Boniface V wrote to his most beloved brother Justus, but did not call himself the servant of the servants of God. He called himself plain "Bonifacius." Justus had told him of his labours, and, it would seem, of some successes; and Boniface commends him. The king, too, Eadbald [1], had written to Boniface, and his letter had shewn how carefully he had been taught by Justus, who had from his first going to Rochester been naturally much connected with Eadbald, then the sub-king residing there [2]. The pope was confident that the work was now really moving on, and would soon attain to large dimensions. He sent to Justus the pallium, not granted, it would seem, to Laurentius, not to Mellitus. They had had no occasion to ordain bishops, rather the reverse indeed, so we shall never know whether without the pallium they would have proceeded to a consecration, as Paulinus did [3]. Justus was ordered [4] only to use the pallium in celebrating the holy mysteries. Boniface conceded also to him the ordinations of bishops, if occasion required. The only occasion that then presented itself was the vacancy at Rochester,

---

[1] Bede uses here another and fuller form of his name, Aduluald, ii. 8.   [2] See p. 114.
[3] See p. 184.   [4] Imperavimus.

for London was hopelessly gone. To Rochester he, alone as it seems, consecrated Romanus; of whom I think nothing is known except that he was drowned in the Mediterranean on a legatary mission from Justus to the pope very soon after his consecration.

How long Justus himself lived we cannot say with certainty, probably only three years as archbishop; but in his time a very great step in advance was auspiciously begun. We are now at last to come to the country of those Yorkshire boys who had set the whole thing going five and thirty years before.

We saw that Edwin, the young son of Ælle of Deira, had been driven out of his kingdom in 588 by Æthelric of Bernicia and his son Ethelfrith, the husband of Edwin's sister. Ethelfrith ruled both kingdoms as one, that is, the eastward half of England between the Humber and the Forth, with York as a capital city, and Bamborough and the rock of Edinburgh as chief fortresses. In the parts about Leeds and Elmet the Britons still held their own. Edwin had escaped to Wales, and the great battle [1] which was so disastrous to the Welsh Christians was fought by the Welsh Britons to protect him against Ethelfrith.

[1] In 613, probably.

Driven from Wales, Edwin had sought a place of refuge with Redwald, king of the East Angles, probably at Rendlesham in Suffolk, possibly at Exning near Newmarket. Redwald entered into peace with him, and promised him protection and safety. There was no man in the island so powerful as Redwald, who had succeeded to the general supremacy left vacant on Ethelbert's death.

Edwin's brother-in-law and bitter enemy sent emissaries to Redwald, demanding that he should be given up; offering large bribes at first, and by a second and third embassy making terrible threats. Ethelfrith was the kind of person to carry out his threats if he could. Redwald promised either to kill Edwin himself or to hand him over to Ethelfrith's messengers; and the information of this was conveyed to Edwin by a trusty friend. It was evening, and Edwin was going to bed. His friend advised him to escape on the instant, and undertook to guide him to a place where he would be safe alike from Redwald and from Ethelfrith. But Edwin refused. He had entered into a pact with Redwald, and he would not believe that a great king would violate his promise. And if it must be so, he would rather perish at the hands of Redwald than be put to death by some meaner person. As for further flight, he was tired of this fugitive life. It had gone on for years. It should go on no longer. So he sat himself down in front of the palace, instead of going to bed, and awaited his fate. Truly these pagan ancestors of ours knew how to set an example to the Italian ancestors of Dr. Benson and Dr. Temple and Dr. Davidson.

In the dead of the night a stranger came, and asked what did he there, seated on a stone, while other people were fast asleep? What did it matter to him, Edwin asked, whether he passed the night in the house or out? The stranger replied that he knew what Edwin's trouble was. "What would he give the man who should persuade Redwald to do him no harm, and not give him up?" "He would give him all he should have it in his power to give." "But what if he assured to him a great kingdom, a fame transcending that of all the kings of the English? What if he should give him counsel for his life and his salvation beyond the utmost that any of his people had ever heard of?" Edwin declared that such a man should guide him as he would. The stranger pressed his hand upon his head and said, "When that sign is repeated, remember." Then soon there came again the trusty friend, to tell him he might go and take his rest in safety: the king's mind was completely changed. The trusty friend was clearly only second in the field. Redwald gave Ethelfrith no time to prepare; he marched upon him, defeated him[1], slew him and his son. Edwin mounted his father's throne, and reigned also over the northern portion, thus wrested from Ethelfrith's line.

Edwin had married, when in exile, Quenburga, a daughter of Cearl, king of the Mercians, by whom he had two sons, Osfrid and Eanfrid. His wife was dead. He sent to Kent, and asked for Eadbald's sister, the daughter of Ethelbert (and, we suppose, of Bertha), by name Ethelberga, or—as her short name was, these people seem all to have had names longer than they were called by—Tatae. Eadbald was now firm in the faith. He said it was not lawful for a Christian woman to marry a heathen man. Edwin, in reply, undertook that he would in no way whatever oppose the Christian faith; and that

---

[1] Near the river Idle in Nottinghamshire, probably near Retford. The armies met in Mercia. Bede says, and he names the river the Idlæ. The date was 616 or 617.

Tatae and all her people should be quite free to worship as Christians. Nay, granted that this faith could be shewn to be more worthy of God than his own, he would certainly not say he would not himself accept it. History repeats itself.

The princess was sent to Edwin, and with her Paulinus, who was consecrated bishop for the purpose on July 21, 625, by Justus of Canterbury. Paulinus was one of the four principal men who were sent by Gregory to help Augustine when the work had grown upon him. There is something of mystery about Paulinus. I am myself more and more inclined to give credence to the tradition that he was of a British family, of the royal race of Rheged, son of Urien, who may have fled to Rome. The name " Paulinus " was a famous name, in its British form, in Wales and in North Britain, as we have seen already [1]. I cannot help thinking that there were in the dales and glens of Yorkshire and Lancashire and Northumbria, specially Lancashire, a large number of Britons still, a preponderating

---

[1] See p. 104. If this supposition is correct, Paulinus's name would correspond with the British Pawl, but he would also be known among the Britons as Rum, or Run, son of Urien.

number, and that to them Paulinus brought the introduction of kinship, and the message of a gospel that had been expelled but was not forgotten. However that may have been, we are told that feeling the risk of contamination which the Christians of the young queen's circle in their spiritual isolation ran, he confirmed them in the faith by daily preaching and celebration of the heavenly sacraments. But his mind was wholly bent upon bringing the heathen nation to Christ; and for this he laboured earnestly, entirely without success.

Edwin was now by very far the most powerful man this island had seen since the Roman times. His kingdom filled the north; his supremacy covered all the land held by Angles or by Saxons, except the little isolated bit of Kent. The West Saxons, who had not been under the lordship of Ethelbert, nor under that of Redwald, were in his supremacy. Their king hated this, and sent people with a poisoned dagger to assassinate him. They struck at Edwin right through the body of Lilla, his best-loved attendant, and the point of the dagger, thus cleansed of its poison, actually reached the king. He was saved.

It was the day which Paulinus and Tatae

called Easter Day. They were at the royal vill on the Derwent, the white river, near the road which runs east from York and crosses the Derwent at Stamford Bridge, somewhere near Aldby, in Lord Londesborough's Park; very near the scene of King Harold's great victory over the Northmen, when, but for their invasion, he would have been putting an end to William of Normandy and his host on the shores of Sussex. That same Easter night, Tatae's first child was born, Eanfled. Paulinus persuaded the king that the safety and comparative painlessness of the birth were due to his prayers. The king, profoundly moved by his own marvellous escape, and profoundly moved by this happy domestic event, declared that if he conquered the West Saxon king, the would-be assassin, he would become a Christian. Meanwhile, he made the infant girl over to Paulinus, and she was baptized, the firstfruits of Northumbria to Christ, with twelve relatives, on the next Whit Sunday, twenty-nine years after her grandfather.

He conquered the West Saxon and returned. From the moment of his promise he had ceased to worship idols, but he delayed the greater step. He desired to know more of the Christian faith, and to discuss the whole matter with his wisest counsellors. And being a man of very great natural sagacity, he frequently sat alone for long periods of time, revolving deep thoughts.

At this conjuncture it was that Edwin and his queen received letters from Boniface V. The letters have been ridiculed as inadequate, but I do not think they deserve that. One thing is noticeable in them, that not a word is said about Rome, or the Roman Church, or any claim upon England. And another thing is noticeable. The pope sets forth the faith to which he invites Edwin to come: there is not a single word or suggestion which Archbishop Benson might not send to a Matabele chieftain. One little matter strikes us as rather out of taste. Gregory had sent presents to Ethelbert, and he said so in his letter; but he left the gifts to speak for themselves, merely describing them as something small. Boniface stolidly sets forth his presents; a shirt and a gold ornament for the king, a silver looking-glass and an ivory gilt comb for the queen. All four were sent as the benediction of their protector, the blessed Peter. It is interesting to note that Boniface made no distinction, as to the protectorate of

Peter, between the Christian woman and the pagan man. It looks as if he was merely using a stock phrase.

The time had come for Paulinus to act upon the design prepared ten years before. The king, still delaying, sat as his wont was silent and alone. Paulinus came to him, laid his hand upon his head, and asked, "Dost thou remember that sign?" The king, trembling with excitement, would have thrown himself at his feet, but he stayed him. Edwin declared himself ready. He would get his chief men together, and see if they would come over with him. Accordingly a great council was called, and we have a careful report of this meeting of the Northumbrian house of peers [1].

The king asked each magnate in turn what he thought of the new doctrines and the new worship. The chief priest Coifi was the first to answer. Coifi may be taken as the type of a cunning priest without convictions, one who serves at the altar that the altar may serve him. "He was anxious that the new doctrines should be more clearly known to them, for he had come to the conclusion that there was no reality in that which he had so far

---

[1] See *The Venerable Bede*, S.P.C.K., pp. 28-33.

professed. No one had been more diligent than he in the worship of the gods, and yet many had more of the king's favour, more of worldly prosperity, than he with all his care for the gods. Had those same gods been good for anything at all, they would, of course, have insured his promotion to a position of pre-eminence. If the king liked the new religion better, after looking into it, by all means let it be adopted." It is only fair to say that Coifi appeared in a much more favourable light in a second speech and in eventual action.

The next speaker was a man of very different mould. It would be well if in all councils in this land there were men with thoughts so just and expressions so happy. He is a type of the thoughtful layman. "What came before life, and what comes after, all is mystery. The life of each man, that is all that each man knows." An apt simile occurred to him, beautiful in its simplicity. It may well have been that he drew it at the moment of speaking from an actual event; for we have been told that long time had elapsed since July, 626, and the king and magnates were baptized at Easter, 627, so that the council was held in winter. This was the simile. "The king and his chief captains and ministers are sitting in council on a dark winter's day; rain and snow without; within, a bright fire in their midst. Suddenly a little bird flies in, a sparrow, in at one door and then out at another. Where it came from none can say, nor whither it has gone. So is the life of man. Clear enough itself, but before it, and after the end thereof, darkness; it may be, storm. If the new doctrine will tell us anything of these mysteries, the before and the after, it is the religion that is wanted." Others supported this view.

Then Coifi became more worthy of himself. He begged that Paulinus might be heard. Paulinus was heard, and was listened to attentively. There were few such orators as he, who could convert a township in a sermon. And nature had given him a form fit for an orator. A certain abbat of Peartaneu[1], a man of singular veracity, Deda by name, told Bede that he had talked with an aged man who was baptized by Paulinus in Trent stream, in the presence of King Edwin. The old man described the eloquent missionary bishop as tall of stature; stooping slightly; with black hair, thin face, nose slender and aquiline,

[1] Parteney, in Lincolnshire. This was a cell to Bardney.

aspect reverend and majestic. This was the man who was brought in to expound before the chief priest of the faith he had come to overthrow, the precepts and the promises of the faith he preached. And this was the result. "I have long known, O king, that there was nothing in our religion; for the more I sought for truth in it the less I found it. And here I freely confess that in this new preaching I find the truth which there I could not find. It gives us life, salvation, and happiness eternal. Let us make haste to abjure and to burn the altars we have consecrated to such poor purposes." All reason for further delay had now disappeared. The king's decision was made. He gave Paulinus licence to preach publicly. He made the announcement that he had himself abandoned idolatry, and that he accepted the faith of Christ. Then he asked Coifi who should set about the destruction of the idols. This was a more serious question for the king than for Coifi. The king had once believed, and he trembled. Coifi had not believed, and he did not tremble. "None so fit as I. I taught the people to worship them. I will destroy them." So he called for a spear and a stallion charger, forbidden things both for a pagan priest, and he galloped up Goodmanham[1] lane, and rode full tilt at the temple door. The people thought him mad; but he pierced the door with his spear, and called on those with him to finish the work of destruction. Then they burned the temple, with its idols and all that was contained within its precincts.

The king and his chiefs were baptized at York on Easter Day, April 12, 627, in the wooden church which Edwin built in honour of St. Peter. Though there had been a British bishop of York, this is the first church on record of the series which has reached its climax in the present glorious Minster. The king at once commenced a church of stone of larger dimensions, enclosing the original oratory[2]; but before the church was finished he was killed in battle at Hethfeld[3], by an army of Britons and pagan Mercians, A.D. 633. He was forty-seven years of age at the time of his death, and had reigned seventeen years.

So long as the king lived, that is, for six years, the work of conversion went on rapidly. Bede tells us of a visit of thirty-six days, paid

---

[1] Near Market Weighton in Yorkshire. Called in Bede's time Godmundingham.
[2] Remains of this church can still be seen in the crypt.
[3] Hatfield, in Yorkshire.

by Paulinus to the king and queen at one of their country seats, during the whole of which time the bishop catechized and baptized. The people flocked from all the neighbouring villages and hamlets to hear him. As soon as they had heard him, they believed. As soon as they believed, he baptized them in the river Glen[1], which ran by. This was in Bernicia. In Deira, we have records of his being often with the king at his seat at Catterick. There, in like manner, he catechized and baptized, the Swale being his laver of regeneration; for in the early infancy of the Church, Bede remarks, oratories and fonts could not be made. We may ask, why? It would seem that Paulinus, in his great power as a persuasive orator, forgot or neglected the less marked but more useful function of an organizer and establisher. Had Bede been able to say that after a time this severe personal work became less necessary on the part of Paulinus, because oratories and fonts were established, and here and there, in an ever-increasing number of places, priests were found, each the centre of a body of true believers and acting as a missionary to the pagans around, we should not have had to record the apostasy

---

[1] At Yeverin, in Glendale.

of the land on the death of the king. It is
related of Edwin, that wherever he found
a good spring of water near a frequented road,
he had a post fixed at the place with a brass
dish chained to it for the use of travellers;
and so strict was his administration of justice
that the dishes remained uninjured. We can
but regret that he did not establish in like
manner supplies of the water of life for his
subjects travelling to another world.

Paulinus left his mark, however, in Northumbria. "Pallins burn" still commemorates
him. An inscription at Dewsbury used to be
said to record his preaching there. In the
time of Edward II the boundary of some land
near Easingwold is described as extending
usque ad cruces Paulini, "to the crosses of
Paulinus." The Cross of Paulinus is still
shown at Whalley, in Lancashire, one of three
remarkable Anglian shafts remaining in that
most interesting churchyard, and the one of
all the early shafts still preserved among us
which most suits by its style that very early
ascription. He made Christians, too, in Lincoln, beginning with a very important success
in the conversion of the governor of the
place, Blaecca; and he, Paulinus or Blaecca,
built there a stone church of remarkable

beauty. Near Leeds, too, he built a church, of wood, it would seem. The pagans burned it; but Bede tells us that the altar, being of stone, was saved, and was in his time preserved in Thryuulf's monastery, in the forest of Elmet.

A very important event took place at Lincoln, perhaps as important, constitutionally, as any of the events of the early English Church. Justus, archbishop of Canterbury, had died. Honorius, the last archbishop of the original mission, succeeded him, and he came to Lincoln to be consecrated by Paulinus. This was years before the pallium was sent to Paulinus, and I cannot find that Paulinus had any commission to consecrate a bishop or a metropolitan. I do not think he needed one; but the fact that he did without it is of much importance. It has been said by a great authority to have been in accordance with Gregory's regulations[1], but I cannot at all see that it was. The consecration took place in the stone church. Paulinus appears to have been the only bishop present. There was in all England not another bishop to be there.

Edwin's zeal led him to endeavour to spread further the knowledge of Christ. He sent

[1] See p. 85.

to his old friends at the court of the East Angles—not the East Saxons, we East Saxon people were persistent in our idolatry for long enough after that—and persuaded King Eorpwald, Redwald's son, to become a Christian. Redwald had made a curious preparation for this. He had actually been baptized, once, on a visit to Kent; but on his return, his queen and counsellors would not hear of Christianity. So he set up in his temple an altar for the Christian sacrifice, and also a little altar for demon victims. King Alduulph used to tell, in Bede's time, that he had seen it when he was a boy. The East Angles, however, relapsed, and Felix, a Burgundian prelate, from whom Flixton and Felixstowe are named, came over from the continent and won them back to Christ.

In 633 Edwin's time came. He was, as I have said, by very far the greatest man of the Anglo-Saxons. There existed, at the same time, a great British chieftain, Caedwalla, who held among the Britons of the west the same kind of supremacy which Edwin held among the Angles and Saxons throughout the east. He was king of the northern part of Wales, and of some parts at least of North Lancashire and of Cumberland, and overlord of all the other princedoms of the British.

Caedwalla and the Britons determined that they must now or never try final conclusions with the enemies of their race and country. The Britons under Caedwalla were of course Christians, as he and Edwin were. One of the kings under Edwin's supremacy, Penda, king of Mercia, a pagan, was supremely jealous of Edwin's overlordship, and he allied himself with Caedwalla. Together they marched upon Edwin, met him, probably near Doncaster, on October 12[1], utterly routed Edwin's army; Nennius, perhaps with British exaggeration, says not a man was saved. Edwin himself was slain. His immediate successors abjured Christianity. Paulinus fled to the south with the widowed queen. All was lost. A day's preaching had converted hundreds. A day's defeat swept the whole thing away. Christianity in the north was gone.

Romanus, bishop of Rochester, had been drowned, as we have seen[2], some time before this. The see had not been filled. Paulinus, "at the request of Archbishop Honorius and

---

[1] The battle of Hastings was October 14.
[2] See p. 169.

King Eadwald," undertook the vacant see, and lived and died bishop of Rochester. Here, though not archbishop, he continued to wear the belated pallium, sent by Pope Honorius as we shall see. It is a noteworthy fact.

Pope Honorius, the contemporary of Archbishop Honorius, was an unfortunate man. He is the pope whose condemnation for heresy by the Sixth General Council, approved by Pope Leo II, is so great a trial to the theory of infallibility. Indeed "Honorius" was not a lucky name for popes; for it was Honorius III who wrote that comical letter to the English, confessing that justice was openly sold or made unnecessarily dear in Rome, and proposing, as the only remedy he could see, that English prebends should be given him to an amount sufficient to set him above the need for such devices to secure an income. Honorius of the seventh century wrote, at the conjuncture which we have now reached, letters to Honorius of Canterbury, June 11, 634, and Edwin the king, not knowing that Edwin had been dead for eight months and Paulinus gone from York. To the dead Edwin he wrote that he was sending two palls to the two metropolitans, Honorius and Paulinus, in order that when either should be called to his

Maker, the other might by this his authority put another bishop into the vacant place. And he ended his letter to the dead king with the words, "May heavenly grace keep your excellency safe." To Honorius he wrote that acting in the place of the blessed Peter, chief of the Apostles, he gave to the two metropolitans—as he supposed them to be—authority for the survivor to consecrate a successor to the one who should die first; for which purpose he sent to each a pallium, that by his authority the one to whose lot it fell might effect an ordination pleasing to God. The long interval of land and sea, he said, had compelled him to condescend to this, that there might be no loss to their churches. This is very different in tone from anything which the sound and sane Gregory wrote. If it offends the national instinct of the English, they may remember that after all this tone was a prelude to a condemnation for heresy. Here, if anywhere, pride had a fall. And the quaint part of it is that Honorius was only archbishop because Paulinus, without authority and without a pall, had consecrated him some six or seven years before. So the authority to consecrate came rather late. If, in the opinion of this pope, the pall was vital, Honorius was not even bishop, and Paulinus had been guilty of the most heinous of offences.

Our tale is done. The Christian labours of Augustine and his companions had to shew as their actual geographical result the little kingdom of Kent alone. There were many stirrings of Christianity in other parts of the land, and the East Angles were once more Christian; but none of that work was done, or was being done, from Kent. Still, in Kent the main battle had been fought and won. The land was to be Christian; there was to be an English Church. That was the battle fought and won by Augustine, under the presiding genius of Gregory. The rest was a matter of time.

When Archbishop Honorius died on September 30, 653, there were four bishops in England. Two of these, Rochester and Dunwich, had the Canterbury consecration; the other two had not. Agilbert of Dorchester had been consecrated by French bishops, and the Celtic Finan of Lindisfarne by Irish. Before the consecration of the next archbishop, Deusdedit, a fifth bishop was added, Cedd of London, who received consecration from Finan and two bishops called in by Finan, certainly not the Canterbury bishops of Rochester and Dunwich. Deusdedit, the first Anglo-Saxon to be archbishop of Canterbury, was consecrated by only one bishop, Ithamar, the first Anglo-Saxon to be an English bishop; and the only bishop whom Deusdedit consecrated was Ithamar's successor at Rochester. The next nine of the English bishops, 655-668, were all consecrated by Lindisfarne, or French, or Irish, or British bishops, not one from Canterbury. Then, in 668, Pope Vitalian consecrated Theodore, and he consecrated the next twenty bishops. The fact that Honorius made no arrangement for the appointment of a successor, and the fact of an interregnum for a year and a half, combine with the abovementioned facts in shewing that the original Canterbury mission had practically come to an end, and Theodore's was a new mission. Of the great work then inaugurated, we may, perhaps, speak next year.

I began by an expression of regret that we were driven into controversial remarks by recent attacks. I will conclude by saying that I have had throughout in mind the spirited preamble to the great Act for restraining Appeals to Rome, passed by the nation in 1533. Its language speaks convincingly, not only to the trained mind of the historian, but also to the national instinct of the Englishman.

"This realm of England is an Empire, and so hath been accepted in the world; governed by one supreme head and king, having the dignity and royal estate of the imperial crown of the same. Unto whom a body politic, compact of all sorts and degrees of people, divided in terms, and by names of spiritualty and temporalty, been bounden and owen to bear, next to God, a natural and humble obedience."

And "when any cause of the law divine happened to come in question, or of spiritual learning, then it was declared, interpreted, and shewed, by that part of the body politic, called the spiritualty, now being usually called the English Church; which always hath been reputed, and also found, of that sort, that both for knowledge, integrity, and sufficiency of number, it hath always been thought, and is also at this hour, sufficient and meet of itself, without the intermeddling of any exterior person or persons, to declare and determine all such doubts, and to administer all such duties, as to their rooms spiritual doth appertain."

CO-CONSECRATORS.

(See page 89.)

THE student of the history of the English Church will always do well to look closely into the wording of the Statutes of Henry VIII. The affairs of England were managed by great men in his days. He himself was a great man, whatever else he may have been or have become in his later years. There were not more learned ecclesiastics anywhere than in England then.

The Roman controversialist, driven off one forged or feeble objection after another to the validity of English Orders, tells us to-day that if William Barlow was not rightly consecrated, Parker, whom he consecrated in 1559, was not a bishop at all. And since, as the Roman controversialist implies, all our Orders flow only from Parker, our Orders are not valid if Barlow was not rightly a bishop. It is not true that the English Orders of to-day flow only from Parker: but that we can pass by. Barlow was assisted in his consecration of Parker by three bishops, all of whom were consecrated even if Barlow was not. They all laid their hands on Parker; each and all said the words of consecration; each and all consecrated Parker.

The only refuge of the Romans of to-day is in the statement that Barlow, the chief consecrator, was the only consecrator; that only the chief consecrator really consecrates; that the others are merely "assistants" or "witnesses," and cannot by any certainty of their own consecration make up for any defect in the consecration of the chief consecrator.

To know what the learned canonists and ecclesiastical authorities of England thought in the time of Henry VIII on this point, now made a vital one by our opponents, we have only to turn to the Statute for Suffragans, 26 Henry VIII, cap. 14. Section vii of that Act is as follows:—

"Provided always, that the bishop that shall nominate the suffragan to the king's highness, or the suffragan himself that shall be nominated, shall provide two bishops or suffragans to consecrate him with the archbishop."

It is notorious that the evidence for Barlow's consecration is at least as strong as that for plenty of bishops, whose consecration is never questioned.

THE PALLIUM.

(See page 91.)

I have spoken of the pall throughout as the material symbol of the most advanced claims of Rome to supremacy of jurisdiction. The important thing, of course, is not the pall, but what the Christian Church meant and understood by it. In considering what really was the meaning of the pall as sent by Gregory, it is of no use to take into account the claims of mediaeval Popes. To do that would be as reasonable as to assign to Gregory the authorship of a treatise on Transubstantiation, or of an argument in favour of the infallibility of the Pope or his claim to the title Universal Bishop. We must fix our attention upon the evidence of Gregory's own time and of his own acts and statements. I owe the facts and the arrangement of the statement which follows to the learning and kindness of the Rev. F. W. Puller:—

The pallium was used in Gregory's time for at least four purposes—

(1) It was sent as a personal mark of honour

to some bishops, not necessarily metropolitans,
without any idea of conveying jurisdiction.
It was in this sense that it was sent to
Syagrius, Bishop of Autun. In his letter to
Syagrius (*Epp.* ix. 108) Gregory implies that
it would not be unfitting that some substantial
privilege should be given along with the
pallium; and he accordingly gives, not jurisdiction, but precedence among the suffragan
sees of the province. Again, nine years after
his accession to the see of Rome, Gregory
sent the pallium (*Epp.* ix. 121) to Leander,
Metropolitan of Seville. The latter had occupied that metropolitical see for more than
twenty years, during sixteen of which he had
been united to Gregory by close ties of friend-
ship, having made his acquaintance at Constantinople. Letters from Gregory to Leander
belonging to the years 591 and 595 (*Epp.*
i. 43, v. 49) are extant; but it was not until
599 that the pallium was sent. Here, at
least, it is clear that in Gregory's eyes a bishop
could be in the full sense a Metropolitan, and
yet have no pall from Rome. It was sent
as a personal mark of favour and friendliness;
and not a hint was given of its carrying with
it any vicarial or metropolitical jurisdiction.

(2) It seems that the pallium was *regularly*

sent in the sixth century to the occupants of at least three suffragan sees within that suburbicarian region in which the Roman Bishop was the sole Metropolitan. Thus Gregory sent it to the Bishops of Syracuse and Messina (*Epp.* vi. 9, 18); and it was regularly given to the Bishops of Ostia, the normal consecrators of the Popes (Duchesne, *Origines du Culte Chrétien*, p. 370).

(3) The pallium was also given to the occupants of certain metropolitical sees, along with a grant, not of metropolitical, but of vicarial, jurisdiction. It was given thus to each Metropolitan Bishop of Arles, at the time when he received a commission to act as Vicar of the Roman See in Gaul (see Greg. *Epp.* v. 53, xi. 64). In the latter of the epistles referred to, Gregory seems to connect the gift of the pallium with the communication of vicarial authority, which authority, by the way, was not much recognised by the Gallican Churches (Duchesne, *Fastes Episcopaux de l'ancienne Gaule*, i. 137–9). Similarly Gregory gives the pallium and vicarial authority to John, Metropolitan of Justiniana Prima. This had been, since the *concordat* between the Emperor Justinian and Pope Vigilius, the vicarial see of one half of

Eastern Illyricum, Thessalonica remaining the vicarial see for the other half (Greg. *Epp.* ii. 23).

(4) From the facts of Gregory's time it would appear that the Popes were then accustomed to send the pallium to all Metropolitans in those parts of the West which since the time of Damasus had been in closest connection with the Roman see, namely, Italy (including Western Illyricum), and also the prefecture of Eastern Illyricum. There is evidence that Gregory sent the pallium, not as a personal favour but as a matter of custom, to the Metropolitan Bishops of Milan, Ravenna, and Salona in Dalmatia; and, in Eastern Illyricum, to the Metropolitans of Corinth in Achaia and Nicopolis in Epirus Vetus (*Epp.* iv. 1; v. 11, 56; ix. 81; v. 57; vi. 8). But there is a marked distinction between the letters sent to these Metropolitans and the letters sent to Arles or Justiniana Prima. In the latter, Gregory distinctly imparts authority. In the former, he is giving a customary mark of honour; he does not say a word about authority. The Metropolitans already had the full metropolitical authority, which belonged to their sees by ancient custom, a custom confirmed by the Council of

Nicaea; but Vergilius of Arles, and John of Justiniana Prima, though they had received at their consecration episcopal jurisdiction over their dioceses, and metropolitical jurisdiction over their provinces, had no vicarial jurisdiction till Gregory gave it to them.

When Gregory was making arrangements for the organisation of the newly-founded English Church, he evidently intended that the Metropolitans both of the Southern and of the Northern province should receive the pall from Rome; that is, the *pallium honoris*. He assigned to Augustine very wide and large powers in the island, to be exercised during his lifetime and then to cease, becoming merged in the two Metropolitans (Greg. *Epp.* xi. 65). There seems to be no trace in Gregory's letters of the idea that metropolitical jurisdiction emanates from the Roman see, and that the pall is the means of conveying it. He certainly did not send the pall to the Metropolitans of Gaul and Spain, nor, as far as is known, to anybody in Africa, but there is no shadow of ground for supposing that he denied the existence of metropolitical jurisdiction in the various Metropolitans of Gaul[1]

[1] Gregory refused to send the pall to Desiderius of Vienne, on the ground that he could find no precedent

and Spain, or of what was really exarchal jurisdiction in the see of Carthage.

As a matter of fact, in Gaul, Spain, and Africa, all bishops wore the pallium; not by any papal gift, but probably by imperial favour (Duchesne, *Origines du Culte Chrétien*, p. 374). This was also the custom throughout the East. In 581 the Council of Mâcon forbade bishops to celebrate "*sine pallio.*"

As bearing on the general subject, it may be well to quote two important notes of the Benedictine editors of Gregory's works. In their note *b* to the fifty-third epistle of the fifth book of Gregory's *Epistles*, they point out that Vergilius of Arles had exercised his metropolitical functions for several years before he received his vicarial pall, and they observe:—"Nondum ergo inducta erat pallii necessitas, nondum ab illo exterioris cultus instrumento potestas ecclesiastica pendebat"[1] (Migne's *Patrol. Lat.*, tom. lxxvii, col. 782). Again, in their note *b* to the eleventh epistle

for sending it to the occupant of that see (*Epp.* ix. 112), although there can be no question that he, no less than his predecessors, recognised the Bishops of Vienne as Metropolitans.

[1] "The theory of the necessity of the pall had not up to that time been introduced; ecclesiastical authority did not as yet depend on that article of external worship."

of the ninth book they say:—" Exinde iis maxime concessus est pallii usus quibus apostolicae vices delegatae, atque etiam aliis, sive metropolitani essent, sive meri episcopi, a quibus in Ecclesiae commodum multum opis sperabatur, quot aut virtutibus, aut nobilitate, aut magna apud reges gratia florerent. Eo nomine Syagrius a Gregorio Mag. pallium obtinuit. Haec fere dandi pallii ratio fuit usque ad Zachariam pontificem. Scilicet ipsius jussu, an. 742, a Bonifacio Moguntino archiepiscopo convocata est synodus, in quâ decretum *ut metropolitani deinceps pallium a sede Romana peterent, et in omnibus sancti Petri praeceptis obsequerentur*, ut scribit Bonifacius ipse Epist. 105, ad Cudbertum Cantuar. archiep. Quae regula per Galliam primum universam, tum per Hispaniam aliasque regiones sensim propagata est, et ab omnibus servari coepit"[1] (cf. *Patrol. Lat.*, tom.

[1] "Thenceforth the use of the pall was permitted to those particularly to whom the apostolic functions were delegated, and to others too, whether Metropolitans or merely bishops, from whom much support was expected for the good of the Church, as many as were prominent for their virtues, their good birth, or their high favour with kings. On this score Syagrius was presented with the pall by Gregory the Great. This was approximately the method of granting the pall until the pontificate of Zacharias. Undoubtedly by his orders, a synod was

lxxvii. coll. 951, 952). The Benedictines in this note distinguish well between the vicarial pall of jurisdiction and the *pallium honoris*. But they do not sufficiently distinguish between the *pallium honoris* given as a personal mark of favour, and the *pallium honoris* given, according to custom, to the Metropolitans of Italy, Illyricum, and England, and also by special privilege to the Bishops of Ostia, Syracuse, and Messina.

convened by Boniface, Archbishop of Mainz, in the year 742, at which it was decreed 'that thereafter Metropolitans should ask for the pall from the headquarters at Rome, and should in all things observe the precepts of St. Peter,' as Boniface himself writes, Epist. 105, to Cuthbert, Archbishop of Canterbury. And this ordinance gradually spread and began to be generally observed, first throughout the whole of Gaul and then in Spain and other districts."

Oxford

HORACE HART, PRINTER TO THE UNIVERSITY

BOOKS BY THE SAME AUTHOR.

LESSONS FROM EARLY ENGLISH CHURCH HISTORY. Post 8vo, cloth boards, 1s. 6d.

THE CHRISTIAN CHURCH IN THESE ISLANDS BEFORE THE COMING OF AUGUSTINE. Post 8vo, cloth boards, 1s. 6d.

THE VENERABLE BEDE. Fcap. 8vo, cloth boards, 2s.

LONDON:
SOCIETY FOR PROMOTING CHRISTIAN KNOWLEDGE,
NORTHUMBERLAND AVENUE, W.C.

PUBLICATIONS

OF THE

SOCIETY FOR

Promoting Christian Knowledge.

THE DAWN OF CIVILIZATION.
(EGYPT AND CHALDÆA.)

By Professor MASPERO. Edited by the Rev. Professor SAYCE. Translated by M. L. McCLURE. With Map and over 470 Illustrations. Demy 4to (approximately). Cloth, bevelled boards, 24s.

HISTORY OF INDIA.

From the Earliest Times to the Present Day. A New and Revised Edition. By Captain L. J. TROTTER. With eight full-page Woodcuts on toned paper, and numerous smaller Woodcuts. Post 8vo. Cloth boards, 6s.

NATURE AND HER SERVANTS;
OR, SKETCHES OF THE ANIMAL KINGDOM.

By the Rev. THEODORE WOOD. With numerous Woodcuts. Large post 8vo. Cloth boards, 5s.

ART PICTURES FROM THE OLD TESTAMENT.

Sunday Readings for the Young. A series of ninety Illustrations from original drawings by Sir F. LEIGHTON, Bart., P.R.A.; Sir E. BURNE JONES, Bart.; E. J. POYNTER, R.A.; G. F. WATTS, R.A.; E. ARMYTAGE, R.A.; F. MADOX BROWN; S. SOLOMON; HOLMAN HUNT, &c. With Letterpress Descriptions by ALEY FOX. Small 4to. Cloth boards, 6s.

BIBLE PLACES; OR, THE TOPOGRAPHY OF THE HOLY LAND.

A succinct account of all the Places, Rivers, and Mountains of the Land of Israel mentioned in the Bible, so far as they have been identified; together with their modern names and historical references. By the Rev. CANON TRISTRAM, D.D., LL.D., F.R.S. With Map. A New and Revised Edition. Crown 8vo. Cloth boards, 4s.

THE LAND OF ISRAEL.

A Journal of Travel in Palestine, undertaken with special reference to its Physical Character. By the Rev. CANON TRISTRAM, D.D., LL.D., F.R.S. Fourth edition, revised. With Maps and numerous Illustrations. Large post 8vo. Cloth boards, 10s. 6d.

THE NATURAL HISTORY OF THE BIBLE.

By the Rev. CANON TRISTRAM, D.D., LL.D., F.R.S. With numerous Woodcuts. Crown 8vo. Cloth boards, 5s.

A HISTORY OF THE JEWISH NATION.

From the Earliest Times to the Present Day. By the late E. H. PALMER, Esq., M.A. With Map of Palestine and numerous Illustrations. Crown 8vo. Cloth boards, 4s.

BRITISH BIRDS IN THEIR HAUNTS.

Being a Popular Account of the Birds which have been observed in the British Isles; their Haunts and Habits; their systematic, common, and provincial Names; together with a Synopsis of Genera; and a brief Summary of Specific Characters. By the late Rev. C. A. JOHNS, B.A., F.L.S. Post 8vo. Cloth boards, 6s.

STAR ATLAS.

Gives all the Stars from 1 to 6.5 magnitude between the North Pole and 34° South Declination, and all Nebulæ and Star Clusters which are visible in telescopes of moderate powers. Translated and adapted from the German of Dr. KLEIN, by the Rev. E. MCCLURE, M.A. New edition brought up to date. Imp. 4to. With eighteen Charts and eighty pages illustrative Letterpress. Cloth boards, 7s. 6d.

THE ART TEACHING OF THE PRIMITIVE CHURCH.

With an Index of Subjects, Historical and Emblematic. By the Rev. R. St. John Tyrwhitt. 5s.

AFRICA, SEEN THROUGH ITS EXPLORERS.

By Charles H. Eden, Esq. With Map and several Illustrations. Crown 8vo. Cloth boards, 5s.

HISTORY OF EARLY CHRISTIAN ART.

By the Rev. E. L. Cutts, D.D. Demy 8vo. Cloth boards, 6s.

AUSTRALIA'S HEROES:

Being a slight Sketch of the most prominent amongst the band of gallant men who devoted their lives and energies to the cause of Science, and the development of the Fifth Continent. By C. H. Eden, Esq. With Map. Crown 8vo. Cloth boards, 3s. 6d.

SOME HEROES OF TRAVEL;

or,

CHAPTERS FROM THE HISTORY OF GEOGRAPHICAL DISCOVERY AND ENTERPRISE.

Compiled and re-written by the late W. H. Davenport Adams, Author of "Great English Churchmen," &c. With Map. Crown 8vo. Cloth boards, 5s.

CHRISTIANS UNDER THE CRESCENT IN ASIA.

By the Rev. Edward L. Cutts, D.D., Author of "Turning Points of Church History," &c. With numerous Illustrations. Post 8vo. Cloth boards, 5s.

MAN AND HIS HANDIWORK.

By the late Rev. J. G. Wood. With about 500 Illustrations. Large post 8vo. Cloth boards, 10s. 6d.

THE FIFTH CONTINENT, WITH THE ADJACENT ISLANDS.

Being an Account of Australia, Tasmania, and New Guinea, with Statistical Information to the latest date. By C. H. EDEN, Esq. With Map. Crown 8vo. Cloth boards, 5s.

FROZEN ASIA: A SKETCH OF MODERN SIBERIA.

By CHARLES H. EDEN, Esq., Author of "Australia's Heroes," &c. With Map. Crown 8vo. Cloth boards, 5s.

HEROES OF THE ARCTIC AND THEIR ADVENTURES.

By FREDERICK WHYMPER, Esq. With Map, eight full-page and numerous small Woodcuts. Crown 8vo. Cloth boards, 2s. 6d.

CHINA.

By Professor ROBERT K. DOUGLAS, of the British Museum. With Map, and eight full-page Illustrations on toned paper, and several Vignettes. Post 8vo. Cloth boards, 5s.

RUSSIA: PAST AND PRESENT.

Adapted from the German of Lankenau and Oelnitz. By Mrs. CHESTER. With Map, and three full-page Woodcuts and Vignettes. Post 8vo. Cloth boards, 5s.

www.ingramcontent.com/pod-product-compliance
Lightning Source LLC
Chambersburg PA
CBHW020902230426
43666CB00008B/1277